THE LIBRARY OF HOLOCAUST TESTIMONIES

Fortuna's Children

Fortuna's Children

PAUL AND IMRE SCHONBERGER

VALLENTINE MITCHELL
LONDON • PORTLAND, OR

First published in 2003 in Great Britain by
VALLENTINE MITCHELL
Crown House, 47 Chase Side, Southgate
London N14 5BP

and in the United States of America by
VALLENTINE MITCHELL
c/o ISBS, 920 NE 58th Avenue, Suite 300
Portland, Oregon, 97213-3786

Website: www.vmbooks.com

British Library Cataloguing in Publication Data

Schonberger, Paul
    Fortuna's children. – (The library of Holocaust testimonies)
    1. Schonberger, Imre. 2. Holocaust, Jewish (1939–1945) – Personal
    narratives. 3. Jews – Hungary – Biography. 4. World War,
    1939–1945 – Conscript labor – Austria – Mistelbach.
    5. Mistelbach (Austria) – History – 20th century
    I. Title II. Schonberger, Imre
    940.5'318'092

ISBN 0-85303-471-0 (paper)
ISSN 1363-3759

Library of Congress Cataloging-in-Publication Data

Schonberger, Paul, 1969–
    Fortuna's children / Paul and Imre Schonberger
        p. cm. – (The library of Holocaust testimonies)
    ISBN 0-85303-471-0 (pbk.)
    1. Schonberger, Imre, 1929– 2. Jews – Hungary – Biography.
    3. Holocaust, Jewish (1939–1945) – Personal narratives. 4. World
    War, 1939–1945 – Conscript labor – Germany – Personal narratives.
    5. Slave labor – Germany. 6. Mistelbach (Austria) – Biography.
    7. Hungary – Biography. I. Schonberger, Imre, 1929– II. Title.
    III. Series.

    DS135.H93F344 2003
    940.53'18'092 – dc21
    [B]   2003044902

Typeset in 11/12.25 Palatino by Frank Cass Publishers Ltd
Printed in Great Britain by MPG Books Ltd, Victoria Square, Bodmin, Cornwall

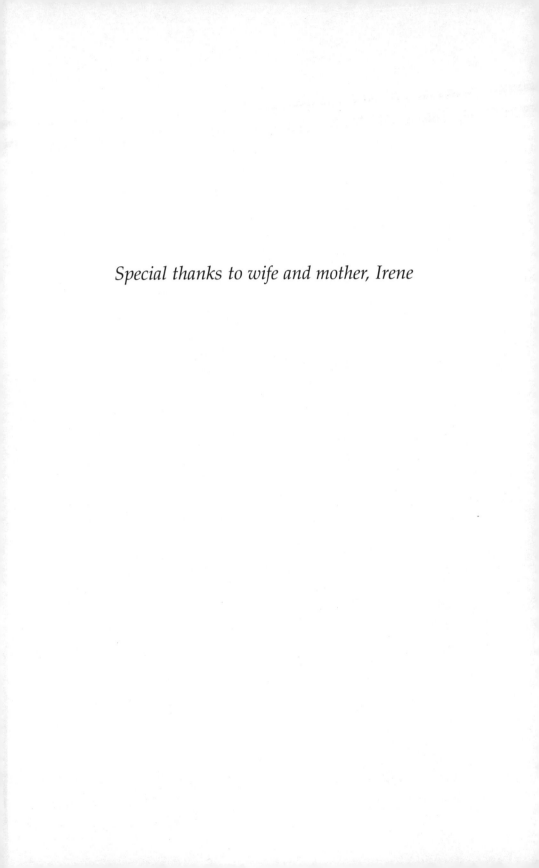

Special thanks to wife and mother, Irene

Contents

List of Illustrations

1. Imre Schonberger wearing US Army surplus clothes a few months after the war, 1946.

2. Hauptplatz before 1900, on the east side: there was a Jewish business in the main square of the town at the turn of the century.

3. The street by the church, in 1905. Imre used to work here in the cemetery.

4. A Nazi rally in Mistelbach during the war (c.1939).

5. The City Hall.

6. Mistelbach synagogue.

7. During the war the square in the middle of the town was renamed Hitlerplatz (Hitler Square).

8. This illustration of the hospital was specially sent to Imre by the museum, as he worked there for a number of months. The sisters were very good and helpful to him during his time there.

9. The sisters of the hospital. When working in the hospital, the nuns wore a white uniform.

10. The army camp, where Imre worked during the winter of 1944/45.

11. The army camp: looking through the main gates.

The Library of Holocaust Testimonies

It is greatly to the credit of Frank Cass that this series of survivors' testimonies is being published in Britain. The need for such a series has been long apparent, where many survivors made their homes.

Since the end of the war in 1945, the terrible events of the Nazi destruction of European Jewry have cast a pall over our time. Six million Jews were murdered within a short period; the few survivors have had to carry in their memories whatever remains of the knowledge of Jewish life in more than a dozen countries, in several thousand towns, in tens of thousands of villages, and in innumerable families. The precious gift of recollection has been the sole memorial for millions of people whose lives were suddenly and brutally cut off.

For many years, individual survivors have published their testimonies. But many more have been reluctant to do so, often because they could not believe that they would find a publisher for their efforts.

In my own work over the past two decades I have been approached by many survivors who had set down their memories in writing, but who did not know how to have them published. I also realized, as I read many dozens of such accounts, how important each account was, in its own way, in recounting aspects of the story that had not been told before, and adding to our understanding of the wide range of human suffering, struggle and aspiration.

With so many people and so many places involved, including many hundreds of camps, it was inevitable that the historians and students of the Holocaust should find it difficult at times to grasp the scale and range of events. The publication of memoirs is therefore an indispensable part of the extension of knowledge, and of public awareness of the crimes that had been committed against a whole people.

Sir Martin Gilbert
Merton College, Oxford

Preface

Fortuna's Children is a bright gem of a book. In the overall context of the Holocaust such a claim might seem bizarre even perverse. One also has to beware of looking for the silver lining, the Schindler list among the schedules of the murdered. Quantitative historians would justly pour scorn on an attempt to find significance in a single life list among the thousands of lists of those marked down for death. Indeed, when it came to those Jews killed on arrival at the extermination camps no one bothered to do any counting. Nonetheless, there is an Avenue of the Righteous at Yad Vashem. There were good Germans. There were even good Austrians. We know about the bad ones from a book that ought to be on everyone's Holocaust reading list, Gordon Horwitz's *In the Shadow of Death: Living Outside the Gates of Mauthausen*. We also know that it was Austrians who played a disproportionately large part in the implementation of Aktion Reinhard and the Final Solution. Many of these movers and doers came from the Burgenland, a border territory that had been a fertile breeding ground of Nazism immediately after the First World War. The good Austrians in *Fortuna's Children*, however, came from Mistelbach in Central Austria. They were good in 1944 and 1945 when they were aware that the war was lost, but I do not think that detracts from their goodness, anymore than does Imre Schonberger.

Compassion is what those who helped Jews had in common. Righteous Gentiles came from all walks of life, held every shade of opinion, were of all classes and either sex and had every kind of background. All commentators agree, the single common denominator was compassion. It was compassion that the citizens of Mistelbach showed towards a 15-year-old Hungarian-Jewish boy who was working in their community as a slave labourer. They were ordinary men, women and children. They were exceptional only in their kindness, if exceptional is the word for what they did. It may not be. This is not a black book, although there are black things in it, like the death of the writer's 95-year-old grandmother in the crowded cattle car that took the family from Hungary to Austria. It is a golden book.

The Holocaust is like Watergate. The more you get into it the worse it gets. During the week that I have been re-reading *Fortuna's Children* I have learned that Dr Six, leader of a special squad detailed to take over 'security police duties' in Moscow under SS Einsatzgruppe B, as well as 'to secure conquered goods, archives, art, and cultural artefacts', appeared in the headquarters of the Fourth Army while it was still to the west of Smolensk in July 1941: he was so impatient to get on with his destructive job. I have also discovered that the cost of a ticket for Germans wishing to watch the execution of Czechs and Slovaks at Brno in September 1941 was three marks: 'German women, in particular, enjoyed the spectacle.' It is because of facts like those that we need a book like this. Mistelbach is less than a hundred kilometres from Brno.

The author and his family were fortunate. They were in the right place at the right time. Yet, what the Austrians of Mistelbach did, they chose to do. Contrast the behaviour of Mistelbach's ordinary policemen with those whom Christopher Browning has made notorious. Contrast the march of life on which Herr Schmidt, formerly of the army and wounded on the Eastern Front, and therefore in April 1945 a commander in the local Home Guard, led his group of Jews to safety without a single casualty, with the death marches described by Goldhagen. There was no pressing reason for a Mother Superior and her nuns to treat a Russian POW and a Jewish slave labourer like human beings. Nor was there any need, even at that late stage of the war for German soldiers to share their food with Jews or to return to them part of a torah scroll used to patch the canvas of their truck. The men, women and children who offered food and drink to the starving and thirsty might have been remembering the Gospel; that, however, renders them no less and no more than human, Christ's admonition to satisfy the wants of those in need being an injunction to be exactly that: human. After all, that is what humane behaviour is, what acts of humanity, as we call them, are. Despite years of government propaganda to the contrary, Jews were human too. And these were not even German Jews; they came from a foreign country.

When the writer got home, for he and his fortunate family still had a home to go to, he was distraught by the loss of his stamp album. Along with everything else in their house it had been stolen. There are more important things lost in this war, his father told him. His son took the point. Nevertheless, Imre's ransacked stamp collection, a collection painstakingly put together in peacetime, also has a point to it. What a small thing, we exclaim with his father, remembering the many unimaginably evil big things that had been done in the Holocaust, but the acts of ordinary kindness done in an extraordinary time by the citizens of Mistelbach were small things too. Perhaps those good people had acquired good habits in peacetime: as Proust is at some pains to tell us, it is habit that ultimately determines the way we behave. Whether it was that, or whether these were people who 'rose to the occasion', who knows? It does not matter. Whereas a stamp album could not be saved, the people of Mistelbach had made their contribution to the salvation of the world.

Colin Richmond

Prologue

In nearly everyone's life there is a certain time which is distinct or dramatic. It is unforgettable for one reason or another. It could be happy or sad, pleasant or difficult. For most of us there is such a time. In my life it was the last year of World War II. It is a long time ago, but I will always remember when I was a boy of fifteen. This year changed my outlook, my view, my character and personality beyond recognition. In just one year a 15-year-old Hungarian country boy became a man. I still remember the warmhearted people of a small Austrian town by the name of Mistelbach-ander-Zaya who never forgot to remain human and helpful towards poor damned people in the dark days of the war. We will always be thankful and will always remember them. Those people mentioned by name are real. Some are still alive and those who are not are still remembered.

It is impossible fully to understand why and at what point in a human being's mind a person becomes something and not someone, and by this diminishing level of respect they become easy to injure or kill. They are no longer a living being with emotions, feelings, memories, friends and relatives. Beginning with comments such as, 'Well, it's because he's a Jew', and continuing with, 'He's a dirty Jew', the rot has begun and is difficult to stop. This is equally true for terms associated with the colour of one's skin or one's parenthood. Many may join in this baiting because of hidden hatreds or fear of others, or they simply turn a blind eye.

However, wherever this behaviour exists there will always be people who stand up to the perpetrators of division. In a small town in the Austrian Lowlands more than 50 years ago, while evil reigned, there lived some such people. They were not conspicuous, but went quietly about their business of showing the better aspects of humanity. They remembered that Jews were human beings with feelings and emotions like everyone else.

This book is dedicated to the thousands of people whose unseen help to others in the most desperate of circumstances goes apparently unnoticed. Those people who do not have the benefit of a movie mogul to film their story, eyewitnesses to ask for an honour on their behalf, or a person to write a book about them. Those who do not ask for praise or recognition but do the decent thing while too many others do nothing, during times of upheaval and crisis. To the quiet heroes and heroines of the past, present and future.

Introduction

KLM's DC8 jetliner landed at Amsterdam airport. It was the first time in my whole life that I had ever been on an aeroplane. The great excitement was over. I was now on my way to Vienna to meet my mother and sister whom I had not seen for so many years. Our rendezvous was the Nordbahnhof railway station. At Amsterdam airport I was to catch another plane to Brussels to meet the express train travelling from Brussels to Vienna. I felt excited and nervous. Would they recognize me after so many years apart? Or would they walk past me, not knowing who I was? I settled down in my seat to while away the long night hours, gazing into the darkness and wondering what the next day would bring.

It was a beautiful summer night in 1961. The train left the Belgian cities behind and sped on its way into Germany through Frankfurt and Stuttgart. Early in the morning we reached Passau by the Austrian border. Vienna was just a few hours away. The train crossed into Austria. Suddenly, I began to remember the first time I had been here, 17 years earlier during the penultimate year of World War II, when all of Austria belonged to Nazi Germany.

I was thinking of tomorrow, when we would visit the town, the streets, the people, if any, who could remember us, and I wondered if the two wooden barns, where we had once lived, were still there.

The train arrived in Vienna at 10.30 the following morning. I collected my bag, left the compartment and then climbed onto the station platform. I looked into the crowd ahead expectantly, searching for the once familiar face of my mother. Suddenly, I recognized her amongst the crowd. I remembered her as a woman of good posture with shoulder-length medium brown hair, slim and serious-looking. At first sight she appeared greyer,

1

smaller in stature and slightly stooped. Nevertheless, I knew her instantly to be my mother. She was accompanied by a young attractive woman, whom I did not recall having met before. All three of us hurried towards each other.

'Mum!' I shouted.

'Imre! My son!' my mother exclaimed, hugging me so hard I could barely breathe. After we had finished hugging she told me who the young woman accompanying her was.

'Imre, this is Eva.'

It was my younger sister, whom I had not seen since she was a child. The last time I had set eyes on Eva her features were sharp and pinched. She had been a skinny little girl with sad eyes and a gaunt expression. Now her face was full and healthy, her dark brown hair thick, while her blue dress showed a figure that no longer spoke of hunger or rations. She was a young married woman in her twenties with two young children of her own.

'I wouldn't have recognized you if I had fallen over you,' Eva said.

'Nor me you,' I replied.

We hugged, kissed and wiped the tears from our eyes.

The three of us left the station and made our way to a Viennese coffee house, for cake, coffee and conversation. We had much to talk about. Irregular correspondence over the years was no substitute for face-to-face contact. I felt relieved that our conversation was not stilted, there were no uncomfortable silences and instead of time putting a barrier between us, it had only made us eager to get to know each other once more. In fact, it seemed as if we had never been apart. My mother was now a pensioner, and because of this and the fact that Eva had left her family behind in Hungary, the Communist authorities granted them both a visa to visit Austria. As a Hungarian refugee I had feared that entering Hungary would incarcerate me there permanently. This was the first real chance we had had to meet since I left my home country.

Eventually, after much chatter, I told my mother and sister that I wanted to take them on a journey. They asked me where we would travel to, but I insisted on telling them our destination only after arriving at the station. They kindly tolerated my secrecy, so I paid the bill and the three of us left the Viennese coffee house.

On reaching Nordbahnhof station, I asked Eva and my mother to wait while I bought the tickets for our trip. I approached the ticket clerk and asked for three tickets to Mistelbach. On receiving them, I looked at the destination on the tickets and vivid memories came flooding back.

Mistelbach is a small country town in the Austrian plains situated about 45 kilometres from Vienna. This was the place where I had been so many years before. But why? How did I get there? I was thinking back, suddenly remembering the little picturesque town with a narrow stream flowing through it. This was the place that would forever be imprinted on my memory from so long ago.

1 A Rude Awakening

In March 1944 my family and I were living in a modest little house in a small Hungarian town called Kiskunhalas. With a population of around 30,000, it was situated in southern Hungary, 140 kilometres south of Budapest, close to the Yugoslavian border.

We were a close-knit family consisting of my mother, father, an older and younger sister, my grandmother and myself. We also had a large extended family. My father, a stocky man with broad shoulders and about 5ft 9ins in height, was a sales representative for a chocolate factory. He had huge biceps and had been a champion wrestler in the Austro-Hungarian armed forces – a man whose mere appearance would deter anyone from provoking an altercation. My mother was a housewife, looking after her husband, children and her mother – our grandmother – a frail and kindly 95-year-old woman. Valerie, my 18-year-old sister, was slim with long chestnut-coloured hair and a dark complexion. She did not resemble anyone in our family, immediate or extended. She had finished going to the high school in Kiskunhalas and was now an apprentice dressmaker. My 10-year-old younger sister, Eva, went to the Jewish primary school in town. I studied in a high school in Budapest and took after my dad, being a well-built 15-year-old. However, I took after my mother, having the same medium-brown hair and blue eyes.

At home, my mother kept a neat and tidy house, while my dad maintained the garden. There grew a huge walnut tree in it that yielded a prolific amount of nuts annually. My mother was an excellent cook, regularly baking cakes from the walnuts that we collected from the tree. My father was a keen gardener, and in the spring and summer the garden was a blaze of colour. He often exchanged plants with our neighbours for honey and freshly laid eggs. The family opposite had a smallholding and

4

kept pigs and chickens. Next door to us our neighbour kept bee-hives, and he always kept us supplied with honey. Everybody knew everybody else. It was an agricultural community in which life was relatively peaceful and stable, despite the war that raged nearby. The ferocity of the conflict had not yet hit us with its full force.

The town's Jewish population of about 500 for the most part got on well with the rest of the townspeople. Kiskunhalas even possessed a Jewish primary school which my older sister and I had been to and which my younger sister now attended. Anti-Semitism did exist, but was limited to name-calling; it did not extend to violence against people or damage to property. After the war began, the name-calling became more frequent and fierce as the impact of fascist propaganda took root, but the nearest I knew of any violence was a bit of hair-pulling. The males of the most religious family of the Kiskunhalas Jewish community had long sideburns known as 'peyas'. When the boys went to the synagogue every Saturday some local non-Jewish youths would run after them, grab them, tug their sideburns, and then run away.

We knew though that our relatively safe existence was pre-carious. Stories from the nearby town of Soltvadkert, whose population of 15,000 was roughly half ethnic German, told of constant beatings and tauntings of local Jews. The community in this town was largely very orthodox, noticeable by the long beards and black clothes of the men. Rumour had it that no Jew was safe alone and wherever they went the proverb, 'safety in numbers', was adhered to.

My school was a prestigious boarding school. As my parents wanted me to have a good education, my Aunt Rene and Uncle Joe had persuaded them to send me to one of only two Jewish high schools in Budapest. Otherwise I would have been sent to the local school in my home town of Kiskunhalas. The boarding school was quite expensive, and as my parents could not afford to pay the whole amount themselves, my Uncle Joe agreed to pay half the school fees.

At that time, the Hungarian school system consisted of pri-mary school for children between the ages of 6 and 10, lower high school for children between the ages of 10 and 14, and upper high school for those aged from 14 to 18. University was

5

for those aged 18 and over. My older sister Valerie was from this age group, but her chances of going to university were negligible. Not only did one need plenty of money for fees and living expenses, but also Hungary operated the *'numerus nullus'* system. This meant that no Jews were allowed entry to tertiary education. *'Numerus nullus'* had been in operation since the beginning of the war and was a development of its predecessor, *'numerus clausus'*. This only allowed the same proportion of Jews to enter university as the proportion they made up of the population as a whole. Jews represented 6 per cent of the Hungarian population, and so the universities were allowed to have only 6 per cent of Jews on their rolls. In addition, top marks and bribery were required. The likelihood of my sister going to university was even more distant, given the simple fact that she was a young woman from the countryside. Few of these people finished high school let alone went to a university in Budapest.

Spring was early that year, but even the lovely sunny days could not diminish the sense of foreboding in the air. The war had been going on now for four and a half years; by this time we were used to rationing and shortages of various everyday items, as well as anti-Jewish laws. However, a decree that even invaded our sitting rooms especially enraged us. Since 1942, Jewish people were forbidden to listen to their radios and had had them confiscated. Luckily, we had decent non-Jewish friends who allowed us to listen to theirs in their homes. There was a regular BBC Hungarian language programme that we tuned into every day, and on it we heard that the war had turned firmly in favour of the Allies. By March 1944, the whole of North Africa was liberated, Allied troops were closing in on Rome, the invasion was expected any time in France and the Red Army had pushed the Germans back. The Allies were definitely winning the war.

As a teenager, new government rulings aimed at Jews did not affect me directly. After all, at my age I did not have a business or career to worry about losing, unlike my Aunt Rene who had lost her job as a teacher in the state school system. I still could live my life much the same as before. This, coupled with the Axis powers losing on all fronts, did not prepare me for what was to happen. While I was always conscious of an undercurrent of anti-Semitism, the subsequent invasion led to a chain of events I could never have imagined. In addition, it ruined any illusion I might have had that the war would end with my family and I escaping largely unscathed.

On 19 March, units of the German army crossed the Hungarian border. With ease, the German armed forces occupied Hungary, which had entered the war on the Axis side in 1941. Thousands of soldiers were fighting in the Soviet Union, but it was not a total war. There were no air raids and no total mobilization. Head of State Admiral Horthy had not obeyed Hitler's orders to hand over Hungarian Jews, although his government had enacted various anti-Jewish laws and taken part in the rounding up of Jews in those lands which the Hungarian army had been fighting on the Eastern Front. The authorities had also forcibly conscripted young Jewish men to the labour service known as the Munkatabor, serving in the Soviet Union. However, the Germans did not find the Hungarian government obedient enough and occupied the country without resistance. They installed a totally pro-German government.

On the afternoon of the invasion, as we were coming home from school, we observed the Germans arriving in Budapest. None of us knew what was going on or suspected what dangers were imminent. All of us were entirely naïve and did not realize the sinister implications of their presence. (We did not know anything about concentration camps or what was happening to Jews inside Germany or occupied Europe. Our knowledge of the labour camps was strictly limited.)

In school next morning the teachers called all the children together and described the situation to us. It was announced that it would be best if all the boys who lived in the country should go home to be with their parents. Our nonchalance of the previous day was suddenly and starkly destroyed. Hundreds of Jewish students from the countryside studied in Budapest in different high schools and colleges. An exodus would soon begin.

The next few days were spent gathering belongings, packing and saying goodbye to friends. Many I would never see again. We all had no idea of what awaited us. Some would meet a terrible fate, while others would be more fortunate.

A few days later the train stations were full of Jewish students trying to get home. On the order of the Nazi government the police stopped and checked the identity cards of all people who were coming and going on the station platform. If they saw any Jewish students in the station they picked them up. They were easily recognizable if not by sight then by checking their papers.

As it was not holiday time the Germans knew that any young travellers were bound to be Jews. The unlucky young men were rounded up and sent to make up work brigades, to fill sandbags or work in air raid shelters or government buildings around the city. However, it was fortunate for me that I did not possess dark hair or a sallow complexion. I decided to take my chance and try to travel back to my home in the countryside that now seemed a million kilometres away. I could not, and dare not, wait for the school holidays to arrive.

On reaching East Budapest railway station (one of three stations serving Budapest), I found a scene of complete chaos. There was hustle and bustle everywhere; loud-voiced German officers were shouting orders all around me as they demanded papers and proof of identity from young Jewish students desperately trying to avoid detection. Each time a Jew was discovered the Germans became more arrogant and nasty. They herded the young men together ready for their imminent departure to the work gangs.

Just then a loud voice roared at me: 'Hey boy! Where are you off to? It isn't Easter yet? Why are you off school?'

I nearly froze then, rooted to the spot, but I forced myself to look round and into the stern face of a big burly German officer. I thanked G-d then that I had blue eyes and brown hair and was not Semitic-looking at all. I tried to appear calm and indifferent as I answered him, although inside I was trembling.

'Excuse me Sir, but I have permission from my headteacher to go home because my father has been taken very ill suddenly and my mother sent for me.'

The officer's manner visibly softened and he said gently, 'All right son. Hurry along then, and I hope he's better soon.'

'Drop dead!' I thought to myself. 'If you knew who I was you would not be wishing my father better or letting me go!' I climbed up into the train and said goodbye to Budapest for a long time.

My father was waiting anxiously for me at Kiskunhalas station and was very relieved and pleased to see me. He had had visions of me being caught like the other young men and sent to dig air raid shelters for weeks.

'Thank G-d you're safe!' he exclaimed. 'I thought you might have been taken away.' Taking one of my bags he said, 'We had better hurry home. Your mother has been very worried. We all have.'

The two of us walked back as fast as we could. As we turned into our street I saw my mother waiting anxiously in the distance. I could see her relieved expression and as I approached, she stretched out her arms to hug me. After our embrace, I walked to the doorway of our house where my grandmother was waiting for me. She too put out her frail arms and we gently hugged each other. All the family was now back together again. Later, my youngster sister Eva arrived home from primary school and my older sister Valerie arrived home from her work as an apprentice dressmaker. They greeted me excitedly. It was nice to be wanted.

Despite the euphoria of my safe arrival I sensed an uneasy atmosphere in the air. The new pro-Nazi government was going to bring in more anti-Jewish legislation any time that would affect everything Jewish people did. We would have to wear yellow stars on our clothes, be restricted to a curfew and only be allowed in certain shops.

It was not long before the new laws for Jews were announced in the papers. They had been enacted on 29 March. Property was to be registered and later confiscated. Every Jewish person had to wear the yellow Star of David on their clothes from the middle of April. I thought it would be strange to appear in the street thus marked out as who, or what, I was. 'What is the reason?' I wondered. We did not have horns or two heads. Why should we be singled out like this just because of our religion? My mother tried to make me feel better. 'It doesn't matter,' she said, 'our neighbours have known us for years as friends. We event went to their daughter's wedding in the protestant church.'

The last days of March went by slowly and then one sunny day in April, on the third to be exact, something happened that I will never forget.

I was pottering about in the garden when I heard a very loud noise coming closer and closer and louder and louder. Then the sirens started. I realized it was the first air raid of the war that had affected us. Dozens of planes darkened the sky. More and more were coming from the south, from the Italian bases. I ran inside and put on the radio in time to hear an announcement about the air raid. I had been listening to it for only a few moments when it fell silent. Thinking we were lucky to be living in a small agricultural town that was of no industrial or military importance, I did not feel afraid at all. However, I remembered the air raid shelter that I had helped my father build in the garden. Momentarily, I thought about taking cover there and asking my mother if we should all go, but then I thought, 'How silly.' Kiskunhalas was an insignificant little town, too small for the Allies to bother with. The planes swarmed across the sky away from us and out of sight.

My mother called me for lunch and once I had finished, sent me out to buy yellow cotton material to make the Star of David that had to be ready for the following week.

When I returned home with the material, my grandmother asked, 'Why has G-d let me live so long in order to see what awful fate would befall us?' She was to repeat this question many more times. However, it was only the beginning of a far more testing period ahead. As a boy, 80 years younger, I asked a similar question. Why was this happening to us? And I was to ask myself this question a hundred, if not a thousand, times more over the coming months.

We did not see the planes return and realized they must have gone in another direction. I left the radio on, waiting for news, but no sound came from it until the evening. Then suddenly the radio started up again with the announcement that enemy planes had bombed Budapest. Eleven hundred people had been killed and many injured in the attack. The names were announced of factories, stations and oil refineries that had been hit. When my father returned home from work he asked quite matter-of-factly, 'Did you see the air raid?' – as if he was asking about a thunderstorm or lightning. His indifference surprised me. I had been amazed by the blackened skies. On second thoughts, he had already seen man's capability to inflict destruction upon himself, when he had fought in the Austro-Hungarian army on the side of Germany during World War I. He had received a bravery decoration for his part in the siege of Belgrade during the Serbian campaign. His past counted for nothing now. According to Nazi ideology, because he was a Jew, he would be treated as the lowest form of life.

Our second air raid occurred on 5 April. Hundreds of Allied planes darkened the sky once more and a few bombs fell on the outskirts of the town where the army barracks were located. We could hear the explosions. I thought about the air raid shelter again. Maybe Kiskunhalas was not so insignificant after all.

The following day a policeman visited our house. He informed us that Jewish school students aged 16 and over from the town had to be assembled by eight o'clock the next morning on the orders of the local authority. My family listened attentively and calmly to him, but once he left the mood changed. My mother panicked.

'What do they need students for? What are they going to do to you? Where are they taking you?' she complained. We all looked at each other and said nothing. I did not know what to say, for I did not know the answers myself.

That evening everybody was very quiet at home. We sat silently with our own thoughts. I was scared. What on earth was going to happen to me? I wondered if I would ever come back. Maybe my family was thinking the same.

The following day, I woke early and joined the other young men who had gathered on the outskirts of town. Everyone had a bewildered look as our group of fresh-faced teenagers was shadowed by Hungarian troops. What did they think we were going to do? What was the point of all of this?

Our group soon discovered what our job was. We were to dig up unexploded bombs. As we were told of our new duties, we looked at each other in horror. The soldiers located them and we dug around them so that they could be defused easily. Luckily, the soil was sandy and we did it very quickly. Our hearts were beating fast as we dug, and we prayed silently to ourselves that the bomb would not explode. I was wondering if this was going to be my new regular work and prayed it was not.

The next day my worries were alleviated. The gang would be digging for bombs in other nearby areas, but had left me out of their number this time. They decided that because I was only 15 I should not have been called out in the first place. Obviously I was delighted at this, and my mother was pleasantly surprised when I returned home early. I told her the news that I did not have to return, and she was thrilled. What about those other poor Jewish boys? They were doing exactly what we all had feared. They would be digging for unexploded bombs for the foreseeable future.

Every three or four days the planes kept on coming. I was getting used to it, watching the planes in the sunshine from the garden. There were articles in the newspapers that stated that the Allied planes dropped pens, pencils, cigars and packets of cigarettes, which, if picked up would blow up in your hands and injure you.

One day I was in town and while crossing the street I saw a packet of cigarettes on the pavement. As they were my father's favourite brand I was tempted to pick them up, although only an hour ago an air raid had taken place. What should I do? Nearby was a cigar shop. Maybe it was from there? Perhaps it had been dropped by the planes? I took a chance and slowly picked it up. It was a real cigarette packet. Someone must have lost it. When I arrived home my poor mother asked me why had I picked it up?

'Hey mum,' I said, 'I don't believe that rubbish in the newspapers!'

I thought to myself, 'What were we allowed to do?' We were not allowed this; we were not allowed that. It was demoralizing. I was fed up with it all.

Soon after this my mother called me in to try on the yellow star, which was ten centimetres long and which had to be stitched onto the left-hand side of our clothing.

'Eve prepared one for all of you,' mother said. 'Tomorrow will be the first day in our lives that we will be marked.'

The next day I had to go to the baker to buy bread, but I felt conspicuous now that I had a prominent yellow star stitched onto my clothes. As I waited in the queue for our quota, I realized that everyone was staring at me. Some were laughing. Some were sneering. Some were silent. Maybe someone felt sorry for me? It was a strange feeling to be a marked man, different from other people, but I looked the same as yesterday, the same as the other Christian boys, the boys I had played with for years and had been to school with. As I walked home from the bakery, I met a friend from lower high school. He was the same age as me but his skinnier build suggested he was younger, with his ill-fitting coat and trousers and his cap slipping over his forehead. I had not noticed him as he passed me on the way home, deep in my own thoughts. He poked me, spoke only a few words and left before I could say 'Hello'.

'I'm sorry. I can't help you. I wish I could.'

I wondered what he meant. Did he mean that he wished I did not have to wear a star to single me out from other people? Or that he wanted to stop the Jews from being singled out for hateful treatment? Maybe others wanted to help as well, but did not have the guts. I thought that it was possible, and this was worrying, that few people cared. That night as I lay in bed and reviewed in my mind the day's events and my new life as a marked man, I thought to myself that there were at least a few nice people left in this world.

The days passed, waiting for something to happen. One day two policemen came to our house with a letter. They said nothing, giving no hint of its contents, and left. My father was at home to receive it. I did not know its contents but looking at his face when he read it, I knew something was very wrong.

'What is it, Dad?' I asked him.

My father showed the letter to my mother. It said that a week from that day we were to pack our suitcases, anything we could carry and get ready for deportation to Germany for work in labour camps. However, the first stop was to be a brick factory in Szeged, Hungary's second largest city, 50 kilometres from Kiskunhalas. From there would be concentrated all the Jewish population of the district who would be later taken to Germany.

My grandmother said, 'I don't care what happens to me. I've lived long enough. I only care for you and the children.'

'As long as we stay together we'll be all right,' my mother interspersed.

The next day and every day until departure, those young Jewish boys not old enough to dig for unexploded bombs had to go to the town hall and fill sandbags by government buildings, stations and the nearby army and gendarmerie camps.

'You go next week, you bastards, but you won't be back!' one gendarme shouted to us on the first day as we worked. The rest just ignored us. They were forbidden to talk to us. I wondered what kind of adult would shout at children in this manner? The world had gone mad. However, despite occasional remarks, we were troubled little for the rest of the week.

The air raid sirens sounded every few days. It became a regular occurrence. The days to our departure went fast. The night before we were set to leave we packed what we could. There were many things from a practical point we could not take: furniture, dishes, linen, the sewing machine, hundreds of books and a whole assortment of other things. We went over to our neighbour, my mother's school friend, Julia, and gave her anything she could put away for us. She did not have a big house and so we could not leave too much.

'When the war is over and you come back everything will be returned to you. Everything will be here,' Julia reassured my mother.

'Thanks Julia. If we don't come back it's all yours. Use everything and remember us sometimes,' my mother replied.

In our minds was the obvious thought. 'Would we come back?' I wanted to leave my large stamp collection with one of my Christian friends, but in the rush I forgot and it was left behind in the house.

'D-Day' arrived, 'Departure Day'. Our feelings were ones of apprehension and sadness that we were leaving. We packed our rucksacks and any hand-luggage we could carry. All of us took two to three bags. My poor grandmother could not carry anything, as she was too old and frail. We were ready just before ten o'clock in the morning, when a civilian escort was scheduled to come for us.

The mood was uneasy and words were few. My grandmother broke the silence, she wailed: 'I am too old, I can't work for the Germans. I wish I could die here. I was born here. I want to die here.'

Our civilian escort arrived promptly at ten o'clock and as we left our home – the home we were born in and had grown up in – the people of our street came to say goodbye. Some came to bid us farewell and genuinely hoped we would return. Others stood in the distance, silent. I wondered whether they were too embarrassed to say goodbye, watching us depart to an unknown future not lifting a finger in dissent or whether they had never wanted us there in the first place. What was undeniably true was that we had become a spectacle, lumbered with baggage and wearing our yellow stars, led away on foot by our escort from a place we had known all our lives. My grandmother, who had lived in Kiskunhalas for 95 years, was taken to an army truck reserved for elderly people.

At first, my home town's Jewish community were herded together and taken to the largest houses of its wealthiest members so they could be picked up from just a handful of places. By coincidence, my immediate family and I found ourselves assembled with countless others in the huge house of my second cousin. From such homes the hundreds of members of Kiskunhalas's Jewish community would be taken away to be transported by rail from the land of their ancestors.

When we finally arrived at the railway station, my grandmother was already there, as was a sizeable portion of the town's Jewish population. Once the rest had arrived, we boarded the regular train to Szeged. It had three extra carriages to take the Jewish community away. How special we were! (But how ominous this was.) The train rolled out of the station, and as we looked back upon our home town, the countryside ahead held for us only a bleak unknown future.

2 Transit and Trucks

It was about a two-hour journey from Kiskunhalas to Szeged, Hungary's second city. The River Tisza ran through it from north to south, and the population was largely reliant upon the fishing industry and agriculture. Szeged's watery connection had even made it famous for its fish soup.

However, it was bricks and not fish that greeted us as the train crawled into this city. We had arrived at a brick factory. It was the largest set of buildings I had ever seen. The factory exported bricks, and this was our new residence. It had its own railway line so we arrived directly. As we climbed down from our train, we joined hundreds of people already there. Eventually, 3,000–4,000 people would take residence here, although it was difficult to estimate. There seemed to be people everywhere.

Gendarmes waiting for the incoming train ushered us into the factory complex. We soon recognized friends and relations. The first to be spotted were my mother's brother Joe, a tall and slim, intellectual-looking man with his round framed spectacles, and his wife Rene, refined and authoritative in appearance. Both lived in Janoshalma, a town 17 kilometres southwest of Kiskunhalas.

Then we bumped into another of my mother's brothers, Eugene, his wife Margaret, their pretty daughter Anna and their 5-year-old granddaughter. Eugene was of similar stocky build to my father, but had a dark complexion that contrasted with his blue eyes. His wife was plump, round-faced, with a sallow complexion and black hair. (She would not have been able to escape that burly German officer on the platform in Budapest.) Eugene and Margaret lived in Baja, a small town 50 kilometres southwest of Kiskunhalas. My Uncle Eugene's two sons-in-law and only son Charles had all been killed in the Soviet Union. They had been conscripted into the Munkatabor, a labour service

16

attached to the army fighting on the Eastern Front, largely made up of Jewish auxiliaries, who wore yellow armbands to denote who they were. Their jobs included road-clearing and digging tank-traps or trenches. They were right behind the front lines and died often due to mistreatment or artillery barrages. Eugene's other daughter, Elizabeth, and her little girl lived in Budapest.

This assembly of Jews was a sight repeated across Europe, but I did not know this at the time. What I did know was that Jews from the surrounding districts were being assembled in one point. Countless Hungarian Jewish communities that had existed for hundreds of years were being ripped up, ripped out and made to gather in transit camps. The Jewish presence in Hungary that had begun 1,900 years earlier was being smashed. We had never lifted a finger to harm our Hungarian neighbours. How could they do this to us?

Families began naturally to gather together and we soon learned that anyone who wished to be with their relations was allowed to be. Our new accommodation was a storehouse for bricks. Huge numbers of people slept in the same building. My parents, sisters and I stayed together, with our uncles, aunts and cousins. Our 'bed' was a straw sack, 'the poor man's mattress', popular at the time with those unfortunate enough not able to afford more comfortable sleeping arrangements. Our lavatory facilities were latrines, ditches dug in the ground and surrounded by a makeshift wooden building. There was no privacy. You had to show your wares to everyone. The only up side was that women and men had separate buildings; we had two flimsy constructions of about 50 metres long each, used as the toilet facilities for thousands. For food we were given two meals a day. There were not enough army plates available to eat from, but luckily we had brought a handful of our own, just in case the need arose. They were a little cumbersome, but in that brick fac-tory very useful items.

On the first morning of our stay in the brick factory transit camp, young men were rounded up and given various odd jobs. I was given work in the kitchen, cleaning and peeling potatoes. They seemed to be endless. Our washing facilities were rudi-mentary, consisting of basins in a wash-house, separated into two for men and women.

My grandmother disliked washing in the basins. Her 95-year-old legs found it difficult to make the journey to the wash-house. There was little water. Even then it was cold, as was the weather. When I could, I stole water from the kitchen, hot and cold, and smuggled it to my grandmother so she could wash in relative privacy. There was more than enough water for cooking needs, but the excess of this precious resource just sat there in the kitchen going unused by anyone. I thought that it could be used well by my poor old grandmother. (This is how my conscience dealt with my theft!)

Despite the fact that it was May, it was still cold. Naturally there was no heating. We had our own blankets and kept warm as best we could, putting our overcoats on top of the blankets at night. One did the best one could.

Life in the transit camp was very boring, just waiting for new developments. We did not know what was happening in the war. No radio or newspapers were allowed. People spoke of their hopes, or what might happen to us. But there was a sense of community in adversity. Time passed, lining up for food or just chatting, and as the days went by we found more familiar faces from the nearby towns.

After staying in the brick factory for a few weeks, we got a sudden sharp shock. One morning, a group of gendarmes herded one part of the camp onto trucks and took those people away. We had had no warning, no hint. We knew that we would be next.

Shortly after their departure, an official gathered a large number of us and said that our section of the factory would have to be ready to leave in a few days. No destination was given. Our time had come, but for what? It is human nature to fear the unknown and we feared it.

A couple of days before we were scheduled to leave, my kitchen duty was turned into clean-up duty. Countless numbers of us began clearing up the brick factory as the thousands of homeless and uprooted people now prepared finally to depart. In one of the bins I was throwing rubbish into, I saw a used newspaper with a word that was still prominent, despite the crumpled state of the paper. The headline was loud and clear in one word of big, bold, letters, 'INVASION'. The article stated that

18

under the cover of shells and bombs, 10,000 Allied planes and 2,000 boats had helped Allied troops land on the beaches of Normandy. Heavy fighting was now taking place, while the Germans promised that not one Allied soldier would remain on continental Europe's soil. This was our only news of the war. The success of the invasion could decide whether we lived or died. What would happen to us? Opinions and conversations were going on all the time. Would the families be allowed to stay together? Where would we go? The older ones had plenty to say, but would not discuss it in front of the young ones. Optimists argued with pessimists, but the children knew nothing. Only hope kept us going. What we did know was that thousands of Allied guns were pounding Nazi Europe.

The day before our departure, in the most desperate fashion, my parents, sisters, uncles and aunts tried to make provision for our journey by removing carrots or potatoes from the soups we were served as meals. They were then wrapped up in handkerchiefs. It was a tiny quantity of food to bother with, and I thought how dreadful it was that our captivity had brought us to this.

Yet another 'D-Day' arrived: 'Deportation Day'. My parents and sisters packed the bags. We were told our destination was a labour camp in Germany. The area of the factory in which bricks were usually loaded onto trains became the place where human cargo boarded cattle-trucks. 'What a way to go to Germany!' I thought. My little sister Eva did not really understand why we were moving or what was going on. She looked lost and bewildered. Many adults appeared the same.

The whole train was divided into three sets of 30 cattle-trucks. Numerous Jews were put in charge of herding us into them. Perhaps these people thought they would escape the fate that awaited us. I only saw treachery. My father, my uncles and I lined up to enter the 30th truck of the first set. The men were separated from the women. Each set allocated trucks for men, women and the sick and old. As we lined up to enter the truck, the man in charge of filing us into it – a broad-shouldered person with a short black beard and wearing a dark grey coat – began shouting at some people who were not properly in line. He was screaming abusively at the men in the queue. A few minutes before, he had been arrogantly giving orders. I did not like it anymore than did my father or uncles. The man was acting like an idiot even at this dark hour. My Uncle Joe turned to my Uncle Eugene and said, 'I'm not being ordered about by this bloody bugger! I'm not staying here! Let's go to the next truck.'

So we promptly walked to the first truck of the second set. This move was to take on an importance we would never have imagined.

There were 72 people in our cattle-truck. It was ironic that in a city notable for its fishing industry we were now squashed like sardines in this shed on wheels. It was difficult to breathe. Most still had their baggage, just as my family did. This made it more unbearable. It would not surprise me if the animal rights movement had had its earliest supporters in those surviving Jews who had experienced these trucks. The crush was indescribable as the smell would soon be.

The old and the sick, divided from the rest of us, were herded about 50 at a time into their cattle-trucks. A nurse accompanied my grandmother. One young person was sent to each truck of the elderly as a kind of minder. Each set of 30 cattle-trucks left at different times. The first set of 30 left earliest and the third set the latest.

Buckets were provided as toilet facilities. (I could not imagine the problem women would have if they were desperate, as it was virtually impossible even to go standing up.) The train stopped three times a day for us to take water and go to the toilet. But we were only allowed to go to the toilet one by one. This time also gave us the opportunity to move about freely and escape the cramped conditions. We were given nothing to eat, and had to manage on the tiny amounts of food we had taken with us from the transit camp. Contact between the men's and women's trucks was forbidden, and so I could not see how my mother, sisters, grandmother and other relatives were managing. Once those doors shut on us we were once again off to our unknown destination.

It is impossible for anyone to imagine what it is like to be taken from one's home against your will, cooped up in a cattle-truck with 71 strangers and not to be told where you are going. (Why had all this been done? Because of who you were born.)

Trying to sleep in a confined space with 71 other people is rather difficult. Everybody lay or slouched on each other. That first evening I was slouched with my eyes shut, making the best I could of the 'sleeping arrangements'. My father must have assumed I was asleep, because he would never have said what he did if he thought I was awake. He was speaking to my Uncle Joe.

'You know, I don't think they're taking us to Germany to work. They're taking us to Germany to kill us.'

I wished I had not overheard this conversation. Now I was filled with fear and apprehension. The intolerable cramped conditions meant sleep was improbable; these words made it impossible. In the darkness of my mind, the same image reappeared throughout that most difficult night, being shot by a squad of German troops in an open field.

Despite our treatment, the thought that we might be murdered had not entered my mind until this point. Why should it? Jews had been victimized and expelled from countries before. Yet who would have even dreamed up the idea and have the brutal arrogance to kill so many? In previous centuries Jews were converted or forced out of a country, as in Spain. This time, the conditions for escape had been removed. Could it be true that those people who were responsible for our deportation did not merely want us transported from their country or our religion expunged, but our lives ended? It was something I pondered as the journey continued.

I stared through an opening in the cattle-truck, watching the towns of Hungary pass into the distance during the day. Budapest, the biggest of Hungary's metropolises, became a mere speck as we headed north. We passed through Kosice, in eastern Czechoslovakia, which lies north on the rail route to Poland. This was my first journey outside Hungary. What a way to start!

It was now obvious that we were not going to Germany. Our destination was pure speculation. Inside the cattle-truck the pessimists and optimists argued. The teenagers kept quiet, letting the adults guess and argue as to where we were going.

Early on the third morning we heard the kind of noises familiar to a large city. We looked out and recognized the bridges of the Danube in Budapest. They had brought us back to Hungary.

21

Why? What was happening? We hoped that we might be staying in Hungary's capital, but the train stopped at Gyor, a Hungarian city half-way between Budapest and Vienna. When the doors opened and we were allowed into the sunlight, the soldiers were asked the same question by just about everyone, 'Where are we going?' They did not know, or pretended not to know. They gave us water and nothing more. Forest surrounded the railway track which, as had often been the case in recent days, was used as a giant lavatory: women to one side and men to the other. Nobody dared run away for fear of reprisals against those left behind, particularly relatives. As I sat down in the forest I felt relieved in more ways than one. Perhaps things would not be so bad. The authorities had said we would be sent to Germany, the train now headed in that direction. I hoped that when our journey had finally ended, we would all arrive at a labour camp to work and not an open field to be murdered.

3 Death in Strasshoff

We arrived in occupied Austria, then part of the German Reich, on a sunny day in the middle of June. Our destination had finally been reached. It was Strasshoff, a town 15 kilometres from Vienna, which doubled as a large transit camp for Hungarian Jews. From here, Jews were sent to work in the surrounding Austrian countryside and in Vienna itself. Factories, farms, government agencies and private companies all sent in requests asking for labour: who they needed, how many and why they were needed. The 'fortunate' ones could leave for their new destinations as forced labour. The unfortunate would be buried in the camp's environs.

The cattle-trucks halted outside Strasshoff concentration camp. It had a railway line leading to it and so again we were 'delivered' directly. It was a former military barracks converted to take thousands of incoming and out-going Jews. As the doors opened and we poured out of the cattle-truck, my first glimpse of the camp was of the barbed wire and watchtowers. It was very grim.

There were hundreds of people now waiting outside the camp, and we were at last permitted to mingle with the women. Once we had found each other, my mother began desperately to search for our grandmother. She was told the cattle-truck with the old and sick was already inside the camp.

My family and I sat around and waited. Conversation was scant. Everyone was drained of energy, both mentally and physically. For days we had eaten a tiny amount of food, had been crushed in a confined space and were unable to wash, while the heat of summer accentuated everything else. Water had been doled out only at the discretion of the soldiers. I was so hungry. I am sure everyone else was too, but nobody complained. Anna's daughter did not make a murmur and sat expressionless with her mother. My little sister was very quiet. She could not understand what we were doing in this strange country, this strange place. My father always said, 'Don't worry, as long as we are together we'll be all right.'

However, things were not all right. In addition to our collective exhaustion and test of stamina, we were all totally demoralized. Not only were we helpless to stop our tormentors, but we had been further debased. Our visits to the toilet had been public displays. Adult and child excreted and urinated into the same bucket. It could only be emptied three times in one day. All our dignity was lost.

As we waited, the Hungarian soldiers who had been with us on our journey left to be relieved by the German army. The troops were Ukrainians who had willingly joined the German armed forces.

The order finally came to assemble and make our way inside the barbed wire of the camp. There were hundreds, possibly thousands of people there. As far as I could tell, the voices and accents were those of Hungarians. Everybody I came into contact with was Jewish. There may have been non-Jews there, or non-Hungarians, but I never met them. The heaving numbers of people were Hungarian Jews from all sorts of places in Hungary.

Barbed wire surrounded various buildings. The soldiers' quarters were built of stone and stood in one corner of the camp. In the corner diagonally opposite was located the soldiers' kitchen and store for ammunition and weapons. In another was the officers' quarters, made of wood or stone. The rest of the camp consisted of flimsy wooden buildings that had the appearance of being made in a hurry, which no doubt they had been. They were the camp's prisoners' quarters. The 'toilet' again consisted of a long wooden building with a tin roof that had an informal ditch. There were two of these buildings, one marked 'MÄNNER' and the other 'FRAUEN' in paint on their sides. In the remaining corner was situated the kitchen and eating hall for the prisoners.

This kitchen dished out 'food' with a tenuous link to the meaning of that word. Bitter black coffee and a piece of bread were served as breakfast. For lunch and dinner we were given soup that contained all sorts of old vegetables. The only difference between lunch and dinner was that for lunch we were given a piece of bread and for dinner we were not. Instead we received a 'treat'. Potatoes were added to the soup for the evening meal.

The washing facilities were very basic and consisted of one outdoor standpipe for a set of barracks. It was summer, so the situation was bearable, but I began to think what on earth would happen during the cold winter? Naturally, it would be time-consuming queuing for water.

The first day at the camp ended with the men being separated from the women. We were shown to a barracks that had about 40 bunk-beds. It was the beginning of some of my most unforgettable moments as a prisoner. The bunk-beds were made of wood. On top, a straw sack acted as a mattress. We still had our luggage and used the blankets we had brought. However, as the beds were made from wood and housed in a wooden building, they attracted bed-bugs, which bit us while we tried to sleep. There seemed to be hundreds, thousands, millions of them. The irritation and frustration was indescribable. The sleep we did get was constantly interrupted, and when we awoke we were covered in huge numbers of tiny flea-type bites. I seemed to itch and scratch half the night.

Our arrival in Strasshoff had made me feel numb inside. From now on I would accept things and not experience any emotion. My feelings were neutral. I was becoming increasingly hardened to our circumstances. Things that would have bothered me once had no effect on me now. It became a permanent state of mind. Only things from one extreme to the other would alter this. Unfortunately for us, the worst extreme arrived too soon.

That first morning, as our family gathered to assess our new environment, my mother's only thought was to search for my grandmother. As we stood outside, huddled together in the morning sun, our chatter suddenly stopped. Heads turned towards some distant Ukrainian guards. They were piling naked lifeless bodies onto an open cart. I moved forward, but my father stopped me. My mother, however, walked towards this spectacle. Even from where I was standing, I could still see two soldiers pick up a body, one by the hands, the other by the legs and throw it onto the other naked bodies. It was my grandmother. She was dead. Piled up were the bodies of most of the old and sick that had journeyed 50 to a cattle-truck. My grandmother had lived for 95 years and this was the way she had to die. She was far away from home and her lifeless body was treated like a slab of meat, to be chucked, dumped, piled upon. My mother had expected this. However, seeing it, the way a distinguished and gentle woman now laid stiff, ungracefully exposed, brought home a horrible reality. It hit us with full force. No news had been good news. At the back of our minds we hoped she would still be alive, even knowing how drained we had become from our journey. Now she lay dead. It was no excuse to say, 'Well she was ninety-five, she's had a long life.' She should not have been there. She should have lived longer. It was no way to treat the living or deceased of any generation, colour or creed. Her body and those of the other dead were dumped into a mass grave outside the camp. The earth swallowed her. Her only journey outside Hungary was to become a stranger, buried in a strange land.

My mother cried all day. We all cried.

Uncle Joe and Uncle Eugene returned to our barracks and, unknown to the guards, took their prayer books from their luggage and said the Jewish prayer for the dead, Kaddish. It became a daily routine.

The second morning we began to look for familiar faces as new people arrived, hoping somehow to make us feel better. Some of my older sister's school friends arrived. I was given some work and joined some other boys and young men cleaning up rubbish and working in the yard. The guards had wooden sticks, which were sometimes employed as a kind of sport if one of our group stopped working, appeared to be tiring or if they thought your work was not good enough. A single 'whack' now and then kept us on our toes. The work was not arduous in normal circumstances, but our food intake and sleep had been little or nothing over the past week or so. In Szeged we had enjoyed enough sleep, but only the bare minimum of food.

Besides this work, time was spent queuing up for water to wash, lining up to eat and chatting with friends. The camp was full of rumours. We did not know where our next destination would be, but hoped it would be better than Strasshoff. My little sister always asked, 'How long will we stay here?' but I could not give her an answer. Nobody knew.

Sometimes incidents had a black comedy element. At night I wandered sometimes into the wrong toilet building. There was no light inside or outside to guide you to the correct one. The building for the women and the building for the men stood next to each other. Once you had finished your business, you came out and discovered you had been in the wrong one. But who cared? The women's and the men's were indistinguishable from each other with the tin roof, wooden walls and the ditch that was dug. Except for the fact that one had 'MÄNNER' painted in black letters and the other 'FRAUEN' (the German words for men and women), there was no distinguishing feature.

One night having just pulled my trousers up, I walked towards the door, opened it and as I turned to close it I noticed another figure squatting in the dark. By the light of the moon I could see a person, who had been squatting just a few metres from me. It was a woman, probably in her thirties. She smiled. I smiled back. In normal circumstances I would have been embarrassed, but now I did not care. I closed the door. But I had been correct, the writing on the building was 'MÄNNER'.

On the sixth day soldiers visited our barracks with a civilian who said he was from a horticulture farm. He asked if anyone wanted to work in the countryside. The men would work in the construction industry and the women in a special place where new types of plants were being created. A group of 25 people would be leaving the following morning. In this case, strangely, the soldiers and civilian specially asked for a group of family and friends. Alternatively, those who wanted to work on a farm could wait for a representative who would visit the following day. The soldiers and the civilian left and promised to return shortly.

My father decided not to wait for tomorrow and we quickly created a group of 24 names – one short of the 25 that had been quoted. The countryside seemed better than being in Strasshoff. For Anna's daughter Sue, anything was better than living a day longer in the camp, as she was beginning to look sickly.

On their return, names were given to the soldiers of our possible group. The other men in our barracks decided to wait for farm work in the hope of receiving extra food, so there was no competition for these 25 places.

Our group consisted of my family (11 in number): my parents, two sisters, myself, Uncle Joe, Aunt Rene, Uncle Eugene and his wife Margaret, their daughter and granddaughter; five men from the town of Soltvadkert, whom we had befriended in the barracks and who slept in the immediate beds; Joe, who was eighteen and who slept in the bunk below mine; his mother, single sister and married sister, brother-in-law and ten-month-old nephew; and a husband and wife who were friends of my mother from Kiskunhalas.

Our group of 24 was confirmed and we were told we would be leaving early the following day. All of us had to be packed and ready to go on a short journey. We were told nothing more. The prospect of leaving excited us. It would be the end of the nightmare and we hoped to be taken somewhere better.

The following morning we were escorted to an open army truck. We were delighted to be leaving. As the truck drove through the gates, the Ukrainian soldiers were burying some of the 'latest arrivals'. It was bizarre. The servants of the Third Reich were burying some of their victims in a mass grave, while people in the same camp were being offered jobs in the relative safety of the countryside. My father surmised that we were going to some kind of place as a 'showpiece' for the Red Cross, to claim how well the Third Reich treated its Jews. He argued that there was no other logical explanation. Our group of 24 happier souls did not care. I looked back on Strasshoff. I had been there only one week, but it had been the worst of my life. My family had escaped, bar one. She would remain buried there forever. Sadly, my grandmother had plenty of company.

4 Mistelbach-ander-Zaya

It took two hours by truck to reach our new 'home'. It was a small Austrian town, 45 kilometres north of Vienna. A stream ran through it by the name of Zaya, from where the town got its name, Mistelbach-ander-Zaya.

The truck stopped at the town station and the driver and his companion got out to have a rest. Both were elderly men in their sixties. It was a warm bright day, and with the green hills that surrounded us it appeared that things had improved. Curious passers-by looked at us as we sat in the open truck. We must have looked a sight! We had not been washed properly for some time, had not been able to change our clothes and had lost weight. We were a rag-taggle bunch of young and old, men, bearded or unshaven, women and children. The luggage we had brought with us only added to our generally disorganized and shabby appearance.

After ten minutes or so of chat, the two men got back into the front of the truck, and we began to pass through the town. It was very tidy and picturesque with well-kept houses. As we drove, we noticed many non-Austrians, probably POWs and Ostarbeiter. The latter were forced civilian labourers from eastern Europe. We were not the only foreigners! Approaching the main square, we could see a large church with a tower and a neat shopping area. Surrounding the main square, streets ran out in every direction and they were full of shops. There were many people around the town.

After about two kilometres, the streets turned into one single road. The countryside was everywhere. In the distance we could see two wooden buildings surrounded by fields and a wire fence. There were no guards. One building was twice the size of the other. Beyond the fence were more fields. These belonged to the local farmers who were growing potatoes in them. We could see figures in the distance working on the land. Those fields on the inside of the fence belonged to the Reichforstgarten. This was a forestry experimental station where certain types of plants were supervised and checked and where the government hoped to create new ones. Workers were needed to tend the fields of dozens of different types of plants. In the front of the buildings, which turned out to be barracks and our living quarters, was a stream. A bridge crossed it connecting the road we were driving along. This road was flanked by forest just opposite the gate to the complex which opened onto the bridge.

Waiting for us at the gate was Herr Brussman. He was the person in charge. He was 63 years old, skinny, of medium height, with brown greying hair. Brussman was too old to be in the army, so in this way he gave service to his country. He was an expert on plants and was responsible to a local town committee and the government. With him was a beautiful young woman by the name of Mitzel. She was tall, 21 years old and had long dark hair. Mitzel was Brussman's assistant and was very friendly. She had a good rapport with my older sister Valerie and we soon nicknamed her Mitzi. It was only to Brussman and Mitzi we were allowed to speak. Contact with anyone else was forbidden and we were only allowed to go to town by special permit.

The five men from Soltvadkert, plus Joe and I, were told that the seven of us would be staying in the smaller of the two wooden buildings. It was simply a barn with hay in it and a single naptha lamp. Everyone else would be staying in the larger building. It too was a barn, though bigger and with a second floor. There was a smaller third building, which we had not seen on our approach, containing coal and tools.

For washing and drinking we had a simple outside standpipe, as in Strasshoff, but the weather was now warmer so we could use the stream for washing ourselves and our clothes. In winter life would be more difficult.

The 'barracks', as I called these two wooden barns and their environs, we all accepted without much thought: what else could one do? They were merely another bare place to stay during captivity. One had to put up with it – there was no choice. Nevertheless, I was apprehensive of what life would be like during the winter. The barn's thin walls offered little protection from the cold. During warm weather, the wooden structure held the appalling prospect of more nocturnal insects such as those I had experienced in Strasshoff.

On our first day we did not have to work. We were given a piece of bread each and some black coffee on arrival. At noon, Joe and I were told to take two large empty milk-cans into town to bring some more food back. Mitzi came with us to show the way. It took about 20 minutes to reach Philipi Netti's restaurant. He was a tall, dark, strong man with a miserable-looking face. Netti was Italian and had been running his restaurant since remaining in Austria after the end of World War I.

Joe and I went to a yard at the back of the restaurant and waited half an hour before he brought out the cans we had given him. One can contained soup and the other potatoes, vegetables and a tiny amount of meat. By the time we returned, the food was cold but palatable. We were all very hungry and in such circumstances almost anything was agreeable.

Every three days our group of 24 was given one kilo of bread each, and Joe and I went to Philipi Netti once a day to get some soup and vegetables. For breakfast we could also have some bitter black coffee. This was our ration and it left our group of 24 very hungry. It was an amount of food which would leave most people eager for more, but we all had to work as well. To supplement our meagre rations we quickly drew up 'territories' in town, in which each person would have 'sole' right to beg for more food. We all agreed not to encroach on the others' 'territory'. This is what we called '*schnorrering*', from the Yiddish for begging. Some people were better at it than others. My dad was not so good, while I seemed to have a knack for it. We would creep out at night when the mood took us and '*schnorrer*', or beg for food. Joe and I had more opportunities to get food as we were the only two who worked outside the camp. Sometimes we would barter with each other.

The most memorable of these occasions was to be months later. At Passover, the Jewish festival near Easter, I had a couple of kilos of potatoes which I exchanged with one of our group, Mr Biederman, for bread. During Passover, bread is forbidden and because he was very orthodox, both of us were happy. I was not so keen on maintaining the letter of Jewish law in such circumstances, but Mr Biederman was. This barter system served us well.

In the Mistelbach camp we received less food than in Strasshoff and had more work to do. Our situation was better only because we now lived in picturesque countryside away from death and brutality, and our opportunity for getting better and larger quantities of food from the nearby town was greatly increased.

As our first day drew to a close and daylight turned to darkness, the seven of us began what would become our traditional evening chat, about our hopes and what we would do after the war or about what had happened during the day. We all agreed that this corner of Austria was far better than the camp we had just left. All seven of us now had some hope, so important for any human being. While we lay in the hay, Mr Biederman, who was 65 but looked older with his long snow-white beard and hair, hoped he would be able to return to Soltvadkert, the town he lived in, located in southern Hungary. He said mournfully, 'I hope G-d will return us all home safely.'

Mr Ziegelman, 64 years old and a short stocky man with a goatee beard, interspersed: 'Those bastards. They said to me, "Go away, you won't be back." They sneered and laughed. Well I'm going to surprise them. I'll be back. I'm waiting for the day to see their faces when I return and they are punished.'

It was something he would repeat many, many more times. His vengeance was fuelled by not knowing where his three daughters were. Mr Ziegelman was a chain-smoker and was always searching for cigarettes to feed his addiction, while he seemed to have a perpetual cold, even during the summer.

Mr Adler was a young and fit-looking 63-year-old, with a round face and a short ginger beard. He had three daughters and a son who had gone missing in the Soviet Union in 1943 while working in the Munkatabor. He hoped his son was still alive, possibly a POW in the Soviet Union, and would be reunited with him and his daughters after the war had ended.

Mr Kiss, who I called Uncle Kiss, was a short, skinny man of 73. He had a son and a wife whom he had been separated from during deportation. While I spoke with him no more than the others, he always seemed a little sad and so I treated him with special care.

Mr Reinitz was in his late forties and had a wife and four

young children. He lived in the same town, Soltvadkert, as Mr Biederman, Mr Ziegelman, Mr Adler and Uncle Kiss, all of whom I first had met in Strasshoff. All had been separated from their wives and children, and all were religious Jews.

Finally, there was Joe. Eighteen years old and of slim build, Joe was the only one of my generation. He was from Uncle Eugene's town, Baja, and helped out in his father's haulage business. His two older sisters, one single and 20, the other married and 30, were staying in the larger barn with his mother, his brother-in-law and his baby nephew. After the war had finished, he wanted to pick up the pieces of his life and begin his father's business again.

As we settled down to sleep that night Mr Biederman had the last word.

'I pray to the Lord He will let me see the day that justice is done.'

And with that thought in all our minds, we fell asleep.

At the beginning of our first full day in the Forstgarten, Brussman explained to us what we were going to do. Joe's mother was to be responsible for looking after the three children and making our breakfast. Everyone else, except for Joe and me, were to work in the Forstgarten. Both of us were to visit the town, although our jobs had not been decided yet. However, for the first week we were also to work in the Forstgarten, and while the two of us were there it was our job to bring food in milk-cans from Philipi Netti's restaurants every day at noon. As we walked through town, we naturally received many stares. It was something I had not noticed the first time, but on subsequent days those staring eyes seemed to increase. Those staring people did not speak to us and we did not speak to them; it was forbidden. We had to get used to strangers. Those people we lived, slept and worked with had been strangers to my family and I; but now as we shared more and more experiences, and discussed the events of the day at night, we grew closer.

On our second night, Brussman brought us a can of naptha for the lamp that was our sole source of light in the barn. After he left, Mr Adler suddenly began to complain:

'I'm a respected wine merchant. How could they dare take me away and leave me like this.'

'Hey, Mr Adler,' I began, 'the Germans have taken away prime ministers, mayors, so many prominent non-Jews. Do you think they care about a Jew from rural Hungary?'

'He's right, Mr Adler,' Joe interrupted.

The young ones were sticking together on that point and had the temerity to say what they thought. Nobody was above being humbled, and that included those who presently held the upper hand.

During that first week, we delighted in washing in the stream that lay about 50 metres from where we slept. Having been torn from our roots and sent from camp to camp over the past couple of months with no opportunities to keep ourselves clean, it was a pleasant relief to revel in the summer sunshine in an almost idyllic setting.

At the end of the week, Joe and I were told that some local builders required extra hands. Both of us would be sent to separate construction companies and be given special permits to work in town and return in the evening. I anticipated that going into the town would give my life in Mistelbach some more variety. Every day I could see new faces and possibly get extra food. I hoped it would be more interesting than digging or transplanting plants, as I had done for the past week.

My new work was to start on Monday, 2 July, but that day was only memorable because of the previous, Sunday, 1 July. It was a rest day for all living at the Forstgarten. It was a beautiful summer afternoon, warm with a gentle breeze. There were hardly any clouds in the blue sky. The green of the surrounding countryside was everywhere. Who would believe a war was in progress? Joe and I were sitting on the grass just inside the fence when air raid sirens sounded to spoil the peace of the day. Suddenly, long silver shapes zoomed overhead. Almost immediately, machine guns rattled, and four dark-bodied German fighters came flying at high speed after the Allied planes. Gazing upwards, I saw my first air battle. My father, a veteran of World War I, told us to come inside in case any stray shrapnel fell down upon us. We came in only to the threshold of the larger barn and looked up to the battle in the sky. Suddenly, two of the German planes were smoking and falling to the ground. They smashed to earth with a sound of thunder and disintegrated on impact into a mushroom cloud of fire and smoke. The remaining two German fighters then became the prey, flying off in the direction of Vienna with the Allied planes in pursuit. This had been my first real taste of the fighting: shootings, explosions and crashes. Joe and I could now return to our day in the sun.

I awoke in the morning, glad to have another job away from the Forstgarten. As I was a stranger in this new town, I received constant stares from the townspeople, so as I walked to work I tried to avoid the main street. I kept to the path that ran alongside the stream, which lay behind the houses. The path turned into a road which ran into the city's central square. From the square, Brussman told me I could easily find the construction company. I assumed the townspeople would be offensive or sneer. How wrong they were to prove me.

At last I arrived at the big yard which had been described to me by Herr Brussman. There were a handful of elderly looking men and a woman in her thirties already present. The woman was Frau Dunkler. In her mid thirties, pleasant-looking with long blonde hair and blue eyes, she was the boss and ran the company alone. The owner, her husband, was serving on the Eastern Front. She was helped by a collection of Austrian men too old to serve in the army.

I was to begin by unloading cement and shovelling gravel. There was no 'Hello', 'What's your name?' or 'How are you doing?' On seeing me there was no hint that I was anyone new. She just gave me my orders and I started straight away. Once enough cement had been unloaded and enough gravel shovelled, I was instructed to tidy up the yard. For lunch, Dunkler informed me that some soup was waiting for me at Philipi Netti's restaurant. It was a few minutes on foot from the construction yard.

On the way home I took the same route I had taken on the way to work, a path that ran parallel to the stream. I passed a house whose door was open and glanced at the doorway, glimpsing a female figure who signalled to me. I stopped and waited on the path. It was about two minutes before a middle-aged woman came out from the house. At first she stood on the threshold and glanced worryingly around. She gestured me to walk forward and I went towards her, meeting her half-way between the path and the door. She handed me a parcel with an apologetic smile, then turned and hurried back into the house, closing the door behind her. That was that. I looked around to see if anyone was about and gave the parcel a quick look. Inside was bread, an apple and a small piece of ham. I was astonished and took it home, thankful that an Austrian, one of the 'enemy', could be so warm-hearted. I did not know that this would be the beginning of many more encounters. I thought if this was still happening in 1944 Austria, humankind was not yet finished. In Hungary we had seen on the newsreels of how the Austrians had happily greeted the German army in 1938. Obviously not every-one agreed on how they treated their conquered populations. Perhaps not every Austrian wanted the Germans in their coun-try. Some people were happy to be part of Hitler's dream, but others did not share its barbarity and still retained the better aspects of humanity.

However, before I could reach the two barns that now housed my family and friends, another side of human nature reared its ugly head. I came across a group of children playing in a field, none of them older than 11 or 12, and one taunted me with the same sentence as I passed by,

'Jude Jude specen hut mutti sagte immer gut.' ['Jew! Jew! You are a spit-pot; this is all you are fit for.']

It was an outburst that spoilt the previous pleasantly surpris-ing episode. I was disappointed but it made me realize that I must maintain my guard.

The food was welcome back at the Forstgarten and while the rabbi might not have condoned the ham (forbidden by Jewish dietary laws), when one has little food and works all day, it was quickly eaten. Anyway, this woman had given me part of her rations and gambled with the fury of a spiteful neighbour if observed. For myself and my immediate family, with whom I shared it, the food was a bounty. It was like being shipwrecked on a desert island, as we divided the bread and ham amongst us all. I had already gobbled down the apple, but as we ate our meagre rations I thought back to a character from *Robinson Crusoe* – 'Man Friday'. I felt sure he would have said, 'Not much, but better than nothing.' We hungrily and excitedly finished our feast. On completion, we went down to the stream to wash ourselves; it was a kind of celebration. The evening was warm and as the water glistened in the light of the setting sun, the woman who had so kindly given me the feast stood in the distance. Perhaps she had seen us in the stream. Maybe she was intrigued by us, but she was a watchful benefactor.

The next morning I left early for work. On my arrival, Dunkler told me a story of how she kept chickens at her home, but that her Polish maid did not like the sight of blood. Could I kill them instead? I had seen how people killed chickens in my home town. First they tied the legs, then the wings and finally cut the throat. The chicken was dead in a few minutes. I did as she asked and was rewarded with a slice of fresh bread and an apple – my second in less than twenty-four hours! 'My luck must have turned,' I thought to myself. I returned to the construction yard to tidy up some wooden planks. After that first occasion, the chicken-killing continued. When Dunkler wanted a chicken killed she asked me to go to her home. The chickens were kept in an allotment nearby and my regular reward became chicken soup with noodles. It was a useful exchange.

A few days after my first chicken kill, I was on my way to work and had reached the town's central square, when a pretty blonde woman in her early twenties brushed by me in the street and placed some money in my jacket pocket. It took me by surprise. My first reaction was to look round and see if anyone had noticed me receiving this gift. Why had she given me the money? What could I do with it? (I was wearing the yellow Star of David on my jacket.) I was forbidden to go into shops, let alone buy anything.

I now wondered if my regular appearance at about the same time every day at the same spot was so easily noticed that someone who had seen me and felt sorry for me had decided to donate money to my cause. However, she obviously did not know I could not use it.

I did not dwell on this too long, and with a sudden impulsiveness I took off my jacket and threw it over my shoulder. Now nobody could tell I was a Jew. My brown hair and blue eyes would be my extra cover. There were thousands of non-Jewish labourers in Austria at the time. They were not forbidden to enter a shop. I would pretend I was a labourer. If someone had seen me take off my jacket with the yellow star attached and they questioned me, I would say it was hot. Anyway, I did not intend to use the money in a nearby shop, I would wait until I had passed through the square.

My heart beat fast. I was both excited and scared at the same time. I would be able to buy some goods! It was something I would not even have thought about as an issue back in March. However, now in July, it seemed tantamount to taking forbidden fruit. I decided upon vegetables as my treat. I passed some shops and eventually arrived at one with carrots for sale. I looked longingly at them. They were fresh. 'When was the last time I had a fresh carrot?' I wondered. 'If I could only get away with this,' I thought. I walked into the shop. The shopkeeper was a middle-aged woman with a few kilos to spare around the waist, despite the rations that war brings.

'Could you give me some carrots please?'

'How many do you want?' she asked.

I reached into my pocket and drew out the money.

'How much does this buy?' I cheekily asked. By the time she had said, 'How much do you want?' I knew I had got away with it.

She weighed out a small amount of carrots and gave them to me. Receiving them gratefully, I put the carrots in my *brotsack* (a canvas shoulder-bag), and gave her the money.

'Bye,' I said.

The shopkeeper did not reply and looked at me strangely. Perhaps she was beginning to suspect something was not quite right, but I was out the door. I felt an amazing sense of achievement and self-satisfaction. My bravery to go shopping had paid dividends.

When I returned to my family in the evening, I showed my mother the contents of my *brotsack*.

'Where did you get those?' she asked.

I told her my story. Again, because I had brought food that would have been unthinkable to get, I was the family's hero. I revelled in it.

5 A Summer of Surprises

In the second week of July, I was sent to help a builder who worked for a separate construction firm. His name was Schulz. He was 65 but looked closer to 75, with his white hair, round shoulders and extremely grumpy expression. Schulz always moaned about something. My job was to mix concrete at the cemetery, putting a concrete frame round fresh graves. He would often criticize me, call me clumsy, stupid or mad, and shout at me for not understanding the special concrete mixture. I naturally took his comments in my stride. I had learnt German at school and was getting increasingly used to different accents, but my knowledge did not extend to understanding the recipe for concrete.

It was not easy work mixing the concrete. (There were no machines to do the job for you.) A large metal tray was placed on the ground and the sand, gravel and cement put in it. The water was then added and I would mix it with a shovel. I brought the cement to Schulz and poured it into a wooden frame, made by Schulz and purpose-built for each grave. Schulz would ensure the correct amount was poured in. Once dry, the wooden frame would be removed and Schulz would smooth it. If someone wanted the mound covered in cement, it was naturally more work and more expensive.

At lunchtime, Schulz would return to his home, which was nearby. The cemetery was in town, about ten minutes from Dunkler's yards. So I headed once again to Philipi Netti's restaurant for some soup. It seemed as if he was some sort of Red Cross kitchen. This increasingly skinny-looking person would pop up everyday for food, while the people back at the Forstgarten barracks would come to Netti for their needs.

I sat in the yard behind Philipi Netti's restaurant, ate my soup and then headed back to the cemetery where I sat amongst the dead until Schulz returned. When air raids sounded I did not run for cover but remained in my place. Who was going to bomb the dead? I felt safe in the graveyard, as if the dead would protect me, somehow preventing bombs flying in my direction.

It was easy to remember acts of kindness. They startled me and stood out in my memory, and I would always think, 'Maybe there is hope for mankind yet.' In the second week at the cemetery, a middle-aged couple called to me as I ate some bread I had brought from the barracks. It was lunchtime and Schulz was at home. They had just placed fresh flowers on a grave. I put the last bit of bread in my mouth, stood up and approached them swallowing it.

'Could you water the flowers and weed the grave?' the man asked.

'Sure,' I replied.

I took some of the water used for mixing the cement, watered the flowers and then took out any weeds surrounding the grave. The couple stood and watched as I did this. When I had finished they said nothing, but took an apple from their shopping and gave it to me.

'Thanks,' I said, and they left.

The days passed one into another as if time did not exist. I had hoped that by working outside the Forstgarten life would be a little more interesting, but it had become mind-numbingly boring. I would mix the concrete, help frame the graves, sit amongst them during lunchtime and work again in the afternoon. A large number of the graves were simply a mound with a wooden cross at the head, stuck in the soil. One grave was typical of the rest of the cemetery. A mound with a wooden cross, it had an inscription on the cross which read, 'Hans Schmidt, our darling son, aged 22, died for our country on the Russian front 5/9/1943. Will always be remembered.'

Some of the dead had their picture in the centre of a wooden cross. All were testimony to a whole generation being killed. A whole generation, on both sides of the ideological divide, brainwashed to kill one another and to murder innocents in the name of a demagogue. The substitution of wooden crosses for gravestones showed evidence of a slaughter so large, that there was neither room nor time to bury the dead any other way.

The cemetery was opposite a row of houses. In the corner house lived an old man with a wooden leg. He often sat out in his garden, watching the world go by. I often wondered why he sat there for so long. His only view was of the cemetery opposite his house. He would watch people walk by and Schulz and me working. One afternoon while Schulz was eating lunch at his home, the old man called out to me:

'Hey boy! Come here!'

I went over to his house and stayed by the gate, which opened onto his garden.

'Wait there,' he said firmly.

He went into his house and a minute or so later he came out carrying some cloth, which clearly had something in it. He handed it to me.

'It's for you,' he told me.

'Thank you,' I said.

Although rather stern, he was another kindhearted soul in this town. Maybe he had felt sorry for me, watching this 15-year-old from his house. Perhaps he thought I had had nothing to eat all day. At lunchtime, I would go away for 20 minutes or so and then return to sit amongst the graves. The rest of the day I worked. Lunch was not even at a fixed time. It could vary from day to day. Besides this, the days were hot and sunny, but I only took a break for water when Schulz wanted to drink. Whatever the reason, I was naturally grateful for the old man's thoughtfulness.

He had not given any furtive look to see if anyone would notice what he was doing. He obviously did not care. I went back to sit amongst the graves. I opened the cloth and inside was ham, an apple and a kind of small cake that I did not recognize. I wrapped it up again and put it in my *brotsack*. I sat and thought to myself that apples and ham seemed to be a popular gift. And then I wondered, where all the pigs and apple trees were, as I had not noticed any. It was one of those things that could keep a bored person's mind ticking over, for a while at least.

August passed slowly working in the cemetery. Joe continued at another construction firm in the town and brought back stories of receiving even more food than I did. Everyone else worked steadily in the Forstgarten. On Sundays we all rested together, and my mother, father, sisters and I often strolled in the nearby forest. On a few occasions we met Yugoslav POWs there. They could not speak very good German, and while my father had served in Serbia during World War I, his Serbo-Croat was not good enough to hold any lengthy conversations. We could never quite understand them properly because of this, but my father said they worked on a nearby farm.

Three men came to fraternize with us regularly. They brought with them some items from their Red Cross packages, which Jews did not receive. They usually gave chocolate to my younger sister Eva, and a few cigarettes to my father. (If only Mr Ziegelman had known of those cigarettes!) When we met them in the forest they seemed eager to speak with us. I waited hopefully for some chocolate, but only Eva and my father profited from these encounters. On one occasion the POWs must have read my thoughts and apparently told my father that they swapped food with locals for chocolate which was difficult to obtain during wartime, no matter who you were. Therefore, the Yugoslavs apologetically said they could not spare any more of their precious Red Cross gift. The amount of food the POWs could receive was considerable and such was the craving for something sweet amongst the locals – most notably the farmers, who could afford to barter – that they were eager to swap.

The harvest arrived in late August. As I walked to and from work every day the farmers showed off their wares, as they would continue to do so until early September. Food appeared to be plentiful and the war had yet to interrupt such a peaceful setting.

One August day I was returning late in the evening. It was still light but dusk approached. The sun was a yellowish glow, surrounded by clouds that had turned orange as daylight faded. The grass swayed gently in the breeze, and some darkening figures worked in the distance on those fields that lay between the end of town and the Forstgarten. A woman in her thirties and her daughter of eight or nine were gathering some potatoes, about a hundred metres from where I was walking along the road that led to the Forstgarten. Suddenly, the little girl noticed me and ran over. Her mother unaware of my presence, continued busily to gather the potatoes.

'Do you want some potatoes?' the little girl asked.

I was touched by her offer. She had noticed me and used her own commonsense to deduce my plight. Her mother had not sent her. She was still gathering potatoes, unaware of her daughter's absence.

'Yes please,' I gently replied.

The girl had long blonde curly hair and bright blue eyes. The Nazi leadership would have been proud of her looks as a 'pure and fine-looking Aryan', but not her actions.

She ran back to her mother and probably asked a question along the lines of: 'Can we give that sad thin boy some food? We have plenty of potatoes.' The mother looked at me curiously for a few seconds, made her daughter hold out her arms and open the apron that she wore and placed some potatoes into it. The daughter then carefully walked over with her open apron filled with potatoes, trying not to drop any. I waited on the road.

'Here you are,' she said.

'Thank you very much; you're very kind,' I replied. I put the potatoes in my *brotsack*, glad of the food and hoping I would have more encounters with thoughtful harvesting farmers.

The following evening, at about the same time, I passed the little girl and her mother once again. This time the mother was talking with an elderly woman while her daughter stood silent, dutifully paying attention to the conversation. The little girl recognized me once more walking along the road towards the barracks. She poked her mother in the lower arm, halting the conversation and bringing the presence of a Jewish youth to her attention for the second consecutive day. Again the mother looked at me with curiosity and I continued on my way towards the barracks. As I intermittently glanced at the three figures in the field, hoping that I would receive some more food, I saw that the mother had indeed surrendered to her daughter. I stopped and waited as the little girl made her way to me with another bundle of potatoes in her apron.

On the third day the mother and her daughter were gone. I thought that perhaps the mother was unwilling to give her harvested potatoes away as gifts every day, but felt she could not say no to the requests of her daughter. However, on the fourth day the mother and daughter team were once again gathering potatoes, and for several days more the same pattern emerged as I returned to the barracks. The little girl always saw me first and asked her mother for potatoes. The mother filled the outstretched apron with potatoes and the girl carefully brought them to me. I gratefully bundled them into my *brotsack*. Once more I was so thankful and astonished that local people were willing and thoughtful enough to provide aid in the guise of food. I wondered if these people gave food as a humanitarian gesture or as individual acts of opposition to the Nazis? Either way, their discovery by an unpleasant neighbour or fervent Nazi ideologue would lead to awful reprisals.

The beginning of September was especially memorable. On a warm afternoon, just after an air raid, I headed back to the Forstgarten barracks early because Schulz was sick. I returned as usual via the town square and along the path that ran parallel to the stream. As I progressed along the path, the fields in the distance and the grass ahead were full of scattered pieces of paper. I assumed that they were leaflets dropped by planes. As I approached, I saw that they were coloured red, white, red – the colour of the Austrian flag. I looked round to see if anyone was in sight. Seeing nobody I bent down and picked one up, hurriedly putting it in my pocket. Then I kept on walking.

At last I reached the Forstgarten gate and reached into my pocket, taking out the piece of paper. It was a leaflet from the Austrian emigrés in London. The leaflet was a few small-sized pages long and entitled '*Rot–Weiss–Rot*' [red–white–red]. In large letters on the first page the headline read, 'The Allied armies reach the gates of Paris.' Near this caption was a picture of Allied tanks rolling through the streets of Rome. It was the first news of the war since I had left Szeged in June. It was great news. The long-awaited invasion was succeeding. I was so excited and ran into the Forstgarten to find my family. My mother saw me first. I was out of breath and caught her by surprise, working near the larger of the two barns. She was shocked by my appearance, panting and excitedly brandishing a wad of paper. She thought I was in trouble – as the worried expression on her face told me. But I smiled.

'Mum! Mum!' (still heaving heavily), 'Look at this!'

I handed her the leaflet. Her surprised and worried expression turned to a smile. Soon everyone came to see what the fuss was about. It was news of hope. Perhaps one day soon our rescue and freedom would come.

The harvest continued to produce a princely abundance. On the way to the cemetery there was a road which had many storehouses along it. These contained grapes. The farmers would bring grapes stacked up high on their four-wheel carts. The storehouses made the grapes into wine. These contained wine barrels four or five metres high, the kind you have to climb a ladder to get to the top. I would watch these carts rattle by in the morning and enviously looked on at this daily sight as my mouth watered. I thought about the dreadful food we received at the barracks and how skinny I had become. (In March, I had been a well-built 15-year-old.)

After three mornings of watching these mountains of grapes roll by, I could bear it no longer. Despite wearing my jacket with the yellow star attached, I asked one of the farmers if he could spare me any grapes. I must have been a pathetic spectacle. I approached a farmer and his cart while it had stopped outside a storehouse. As I held out my hand, I gestured, opening my palm and pointing at the same time in the direction of the mountain of grapes. (I was sure my face had gone bright red!) I nearly choked on my words:

'Could I have a few please?'

The farmer's face was expressionless. He showed no surprise but made no attempt to chase me away. He looked at my yellow star, looked me up and down and then reached for some grapes. I felt a sigh of relief and I must have beamed him a smile. He opened my *brotsack*, smiled as he dug his hand into the mountain of grapes, and put two handfuls inside it.

'Thanks,' I said, startled.

`I left him with my head down, trying to avoid the world. I was shocked. I had genuinely assumed he would tell me to go away, but I was very happy and pleased with myself.

I arrived home that evening and again I went to my mother to show my bounty.

'Mum, look what I've got in my bag,' I said excitedly.

I opened my *brotsack* and she peered in. Her mouth opened and she said nothing for about ten seconds.

'What on earth have you got there?' was her astonished

response. (She could not believe her eyes.)

'Mum, don't you recognize grapes anymore?' I said cheekily. She laughed and I gave her my *brotsack*.

That evening my family sat eating our miraculous grapes outside on the grass under the moonlight. Suddenly, the night sky lit up and all the horizon became bright. The light rose further and fell. It flickered, rising and falling again. Allied bombers had bombed the Zisterdorf oil refinery, about 25 kilometres away. The burning oil lit the evening sky for miles around and would continue to be seen for two more days. It was a paradox. Most of Europe was rationing its food while we sat in the Forstgarten with the bare essentials of life for comfort, surrounded by idyllic countryside and eating our feast of grapes by the light of Armageddon.

Two days later I tried obtaining grapes again. This time I had less hesitation and less guilt. The farmer must have given me more than a kilo of grapes. Every morning I waited to see if a different farmer was delivering any, and I would ask him for some. If a farmer appeared who had already given previously, then I did not bother. It became easier each time for me to have the courage to ask. Almost every other day, for a two-week period, my family were delighted with the August harvest. On one occasion I received about two kilos of grapes, but usually the amount was however many my hands could hold when the farmer gave them to me. I can honestly say that I have never eaten so many grapes in such a short period of time. Once I saw that the farmers were willing to give me grapes, I kept on going back for more. Here were yet more paradoxes. Food was rationed, but wine was made. The local Austrians ate little fruit, but the slave labourers ate grapes for a fortnight. It seemed odd that while we were fed such meagre, poor-quality food, the only source of extra nutrition at this time that I could get my hands on was a fruit coveted by the ancient Romans as the food of the gods. Unfortunately, the grape harvest could not last forever, and so our feasting ended.

6 Nazis Too Close for Comfort

Schulz was sick on and off for a number of weeks in late August and early September. It was some kind of flu and he seemed pretty bad. All 24 of us at the Forstgarten had so far escaped illness. We were undoubtedly thinner, but had yet to catch any colds or have any other kind of sickness that might warrant medical attention. Despite poor nutrition, we had been lucky so far.

I turned up for work one September day, but Schulz did not arrive. I waited and waited. Finally a grave-digger, whose house was one of those that ran parallel to the cemetery, came out to tell me that Schulz was not turning up. He would be at home for a few days. The grave-digger was in his seventies, short and with the kind of curved spine which indicated he had been doing the job for a long time. (It was not the career that I hoped for!) He told me he was very busy and he needed my help. Two SS men and a locomotive driver had been killed outside the town when Allied fighter planes had machine-gunned the train on which they had been travelling. The driver was a local man, but the SS soldiers were from eastern Germany. The SS troops would be buried in the town where they had died. The graves had to be dug by the following day. There was going to be a large army funeral with music.

I alone dug the graves. When the old grave-digger had told me he needed assistance, what he had in fact meant was that I would do the work alone. (I could not help thinking that at his age he probably did not want to be too close to a grave!)

It took me all day to dig the three, two-metre-deep graves. It was difficult work, but you had to do as you were told. I was given a small ladder so I could climb out of the hole I had dug. As I dug in the first hole, I found a bone. I did not know if it was an animal bone or from a person who had been buried previously. I waited until I had dug deep enough and then covered the bone. Nevertheless, it did not worry me unduly or make me feel eerie about working in a cemetery. Since March my horizons had changed. Anyway, in this case, it was on whose behalf you dug for that counted. I was not digging a grave for someone I knew; I was digging for two SS soldiers. I would rather dig their graves than they dig mine! (Not many Jews had had such a pleasure.)

The next morning a guard of honour brought the two SS soldiers' coffins. They were covered in Nazi flags – the infamous red background with the black swastika in the centre. A band played the music. There were many guests. The guard of honour prepared themselves to shoot some volleys over the dead. I stood far in the distance. As I moved forward to get a better look, the old grave-digger who stood with me said:

'A Jew isn't wanted at an SS funeral. Stay out of sight!'

It was firm but useful advice.

After the funeral had finished and the guests had left, we waited half an hour before approaching the graves. I assumed we had waited to ensure everyone had long gone. As I shovelled the dirt onto the coffins I thought about what the old grave-digger had said. Imagine if those guests had known who would be digging the graves and burying the bodies? Those soldiers who now lay dead in the coffins would never have expected such a fate. It was a fate the SS themselves had handed out to Jews, I had no doubt. It was possible that the men in the caskets had committed crimes against Jews. Then I remembered something Mr Adler had said about being taken from his home and what I had thought at the time. Nobody was above being humbled, and that included those who presently held the upper hand.

In the first week of October, Schulz and I had to go to a butter factory to replace a few tiles. We arrived in the afternoon after a morning in the cemetery. The whole job took about an hour but by the time we had finished it was dusk. After finishing I asked Schulz if I could have a drink of water. He then went to the manager of the factory to ask on my behalf. The factory manager wore a large swastika on his chest and was inspecting our completed work. I was told to go through to the plant's floor and out through to a standpipe at the back of the factory. It was a medium-sized factory with piles and piles of butter, as you would expect in a butter factory. As I walked into the plant, a young woman in her late teens or early twenties was standing and patting a pile of butter. She was alone in the room. As I made my way to the door which led to the back of the factory, the woman suddenly called out to me,

'Wait.'

I was startled and turned to look in her direction.

'Quickly!'

Her voice had a desperate urgency, but I did not understand what she had meant. Suddenly, she scraped some butter from the large pile she had been patting, put it into some paper and wrapped it up. The young woman then stepped forward and shoved it into the pocket of my jacket. (It must have been about half a kilo of butter.)

'Thanks,' was my shocked reaction. I gaped. Once again I could not believe my luck. The yellow piles of butter had appeared like gold ingots before my eyes – an inaccessible treasure. Now I actually had some!

Before leaving, the factory manager and Schulz stood on the factory floor chatting. I remained near the door at the front and waited. The young woman gave me a quick glance and smiled while she endlessly patted the butter. I smiled back. Just then Schultz walked over. He had been given a present by the manager, about a quarter kilo of butter. Schulz then gave me a strange look. He returned to speak to the manager and pointed in the direction of the girl. I thought he had caught us exchanging glances and could not believe he had actually snitched on me! The manager and Schulz went over to the woman. There was a short conversation. I looked down at the floor, pretending not to notice what was going on. Schulz then walked over. All I could see was his feet as my eyes were set firmly on the ground. I lifted my head and there in his hands was some butter! About a quarter kilo. Schulz had seen nothing! He had asked, on my behalf, the manager sporting the swastika for some butter, and he had got it!

'Thank you!'

I exaggerated my gratitude, but I was glad all the same. Now I had a double bonus!

On my way back to the barracks I decided, as I had been doubly lucky, that I would eat, there and then, the butter given to me by Schulz. (I was that hungry!) The rest I would save for my family. Before I reached the bridge, I pulled pieces from the butter, placed them in my mouth and did my best to eat them. I arrived back in the Forstgarten with about half a kilo of butter left. It was shared out amongst my family, and we all spread it on the tasteless bread we ate each morning. They could not believe it! And I could not believe how ill I felt later that evening. It suddenly hit me – a bolt from the blue. I felt terribly sick. I decided that either Schulz and the butter factory manager had poisoned me, or that eating large amounts of butter on its own was not good for you, especially on an empty stomach. I decided upon the latter.

A few days later, the glass in the naptha lamp in our barn broke. We told Brussman that we needed a new one, but he replied that it would take a few weeks. As it was our only source of light, a few weeks was too long. We all knew it would be difficult to obtain another lamp as a war was in progress. However, a naptha lamp had been in use before Thomas Edison had invented the electric light, and so I hoped I would be able to buy one in town. On my way to the cemetery one morning, I passed the largest glass shop in town. I had some money from my *schnorrering* activities and intended to buy a lamp glass if the shop had one. I took off my jacket and threw it over my shoulder. As I walked into the shop, a customer greeted the shopkeeper, '*Heil Hitler!*' he said.

The shop was covered in mirrors and adorning its walls were pictures of Göring and Himmler. It did not take much to realize that the owners were keen Nazis. Despite seeing those newsreels of the Viennese people excitedly greeting Hitler in 1938, it was the first time I had seen such a display of Nazi affection amongst the townspeople of Mistelbach. Whether more illustrations of such affection towards the Nazis or pictures of them adorning shop walls existed, I did not know.

My initial reaction was one of fearful shock. Then as I approached the counter I exclaimed: '*Heil Hitler!*'

'What do you wish to buy?' the lady behind the counter asked.

'A lamp glass,' I replied.

'What size?'

'I'm not sure. I need either a size eight or ten.'

'Well, I can sell you both.'

She handed me a size-eight lamp glass and also a size ten. I hurriedly paid her for the two and left.

On my return to the barracks, my companions gave me a hero's welcome. They laughed at my *'Heil Hitler'* story. Such a simple item to obtain before the war was now so treasured. As it turned out the size we needed was in fact eight. I had had yet another 'adventure' story to tell. Each time I received another ovation for my audacity, it gave me the confidence to do it again. I was beginning to think of myself as everyone's saviour and started to believe it was now my job to look after 'my flock'. They were my responsibility.

Whenever I had some money I would go shopping. This might seem obvious, but if you are forbidden to shop it was a risk. When I first began *schnorrering*, I covered my yellow star, thinking that those people whose doors I knocked upon would assume I was a slave labourer and not a Jew. I could not take the chance of unveiling the Star of David in case I came across a Nazi sympathizer. It was one matter being told to get lost for begging as a non-Jewish labourer, but another as a Jew. A Nazi sympathizer would call the police for a Jew, I was certain of that. I would possibly be shot. However, my 'territory' encompassed those houses near our barracks. Every day I passed these homes, mostly housing farmers, on my return from work, and my yellow star was visible to anyone who saw me. Therefore, as I became more confident and met my neighbours regularly, I assumed they knew I was Jewish. The Forstgarten was only a few hundred metres away. No longer did I bother hiding the symbol of who I was, because those people in my 'patch' must have known. However, I would never have dared to *schnorrer* deeper in town. Those living on the outskirts were less conspicuous, so could give help in the form of food or money, and I could receive it obtrusively. Everyone at the Forstgarten barracks kept their own 'territory' on the edge of town, so as to be as discreet as possible. Whether the majority of Mistelbach's population was prepared to offer assistance I did not know. Nevertheless, those townspeople who were willing to give to their Jewish beggars were not obliged. They could have caused us trouble. But they did not. They did the decent thing, either by telling us politely they had nothing to offer or by actually providing some gift.

Whenever I visited a shop I would always take off my jacket with the yellow star attached. It was dangerous naturally, but each time I got away with it the next time was easier. The shopkeepers knew I was not German, but they had no problem in serving someone they thought was a foreign labourer. To coin a cliché, 'Business was business.'

One dark and dank day in early October I was not so lucky. I went to the shop where I had bought carrots and which I had visited on several other occasions. I walked into the shop and instead of the plump lady, a man stood amongst the vegetables. He looked at me and scowled, 'You bloody Jew! What are you doing in here!'

I did not think twice, and ran from the shop. He was swearing and cursing as he followed me outside. His abuse quickly faded in the distance as I ran until I had turned the street corner. However, I did not want to be seen running through the streets: that would look suspicious. Therefore, I composed myself and walked as usual the rest of the way to work, putting back on my jacket with the yellow star attached. I kept glancing over my shoulder in case the man had called the police, but I was safe.

As I reached the road to the cemetery, a small boy approached me and gave me an apple.

'Thanks,' I said and smiled at him.

The boy smiled back. Then again we knew each other well. Along this road were some basement flats. Anyone walking along the street was visible to those people dwelling in them. They were certainly visible to me. In one of them lived a woman of about forty with her young son, around nine or ten years old. Twice a week, she would send out her son to give me a gift of food. One day it would be a sandwich, another an apple and another a bun. I had stopped near her basement flat by chance while tying my laces one day. She had seen me, and I saw her as I looked up after finishing the final knot. The following day she had sent out her son to give me a sandwich. 'This is from the lady in the window,' the boy had told me, and so I assumed it was the person whose face I had seen peering from a basement flat the day before.

There was no doubt in my mind that there were people in this town who disliked the Nazis' harsh treatment of their fellow human beings and were willing to do something about it. They were not prepared to be outspoken or to fight, but at least in Mistelbach some people were decent. I knew that.

7 A Light in the Darkness

In the last week of October, Brussman announced that there was going to be a big clean up at the Forstgarten. The summer had turned into autumn, and the days and nights had grown colder. Leaves littered the ground and the green and blue of summer had been replaced by the brown, orange and grey of autumn. The nights were now increasingly uncomfortable as we tried to keep warm. The coldest time of year was yet to come. I still had the blankets I had brought with me from Kiskunhalas. All 24 of us had packed blankets in the luggage we had been allowed to take. They were to prove the most useful items anyone of us had packed.

Our group of 24 had increased to 27. The brother and sister whom we had met in Strasshoff had joined us. They had brought their mother who was in her seventies but had survived the cattle truck that had killed my grandmother. She was very resilient and had survived another camp before coming to Mistelbach along with her children. All three had arrived on the same train into Strasshoff as my family and me. The daughter, Sarah, an excellent doctor, was an extremely plump woman. The past few months had not dented her huge frame. Her brother was a less conspicuous character. Of slim build and medium height, he had begun studying to be a lawyer when Jews suddenly found themselves barred from universities. The mother found herself helping to look after my cousin Anna's daughter and Joe's baby nephew. Her son and daughter were to work in the Forstgarten.

Our last Sunday of October was spent cleaning up the barracks, raking the paths and brushing up the leaves of the Forstgarten. Everything was tidied and neatly placed. We knew some guests were coming but did not know who; we asked Brussman about them, but he was drunk and insulted us. Sometimes he would come to work intoxicated and become verbally abusive. However, when he was sober, which was most of the time, he was fair, though he said little.

Sunday was usually a rest day but our guests were obviously important. We started guessing who they would be and waited for the next day. Mr Biederman, Mr Ziegelman and Uncle Kiss were pessimistic. They speculated that we might be leaving and going to a worse place than our present one. (These older men rarely looked on the bright side of life. Perhaps it was their age.) I did not agree with their pessimistic view. However, there were some restless souls in our barn that night.

The following morning, several elegant-looking civilians, who were Red Cross representatives, and some German officers arrived at the Fortsgarten. I was at work in the cemetery when they arrived. My father told me they looked around the barracks for about 15 minutes and later took a walk in the nearby countryside. The German officers explained to them what we did and told them we had doctors. Then, after a discussion amongst the German officers and the Red Cross representatives, they all left. My father had guessed that we had been brought to Mistelbach to be part of a Red Cross 'showpiece' camp, and this episode illustrated that he might well have been correct.

The German officers had no doubt told the representatives the rumours were false, the Germans were not so bad to the Jews. I expect they told them, 'Look, they have such beautiful countryside to live in. Their living quarters are basic, but think of our troops on the Eastern Front. Their work isn't so difficult or degrading. They live a decent life.' We had to be grateful for small mercies, but they had not told them of the tiny amount of food we received which led us to beg in town. Did the Red Cross representatives know that we had been forcibly uprooted from our own country, moved and made to work on behalf of the German Reich against our will? Had the officers told them we had been forced to travel more than 70 to a truck on a train with no food and their forces had buried the dead in mass graves, just a stone's throw from where we slept? None of this had been said. And did the Red Cross really care?

Some days after the visit of the Red Cross representatives, Frau Dunkler sent for me. Schulz was by now constantly sick with what was said to be the flu. Dunkler herself was going away. This meant there was no one left to supervise me. Therefore, I was to be sent to the town hospital to feed coal to the central heating system; two men were needed to work it. Usually a Russian POW and an Austrian worked there, but the latter had been sent on war duty and so I was to take his place.

The first day was very bad and I wondered how I could survive. The Russian POW and I had to carry bag after bag of coal from the train cars to the trucks parked at the station. The locomotive was marked, 'Radchen fahren bis zum sieg' [The wheels are rolling towards victory]. The coal was for the hospital heating system. Each bag seemed to weigh heavier than the last. Being only fifteen at the time, I was ready to drop at noon. I assumed that from now on this was my new job. How could I survive this every day? I could barely survive half a day. However, I pulled through because I had to. It is amazing what you can do when there is no alternative.

It was not only the back-breaking work which was the problem. In war, a railway station is one of the worst places to be. Air raids happened every day. Stations were bombed. I personally had buried the dead of an attack on a train. Supplies such as oil and coal were prime targets. I worried that pilots would be able to see the coal from their planes and attack us. This weighed upon my mind as the coal weighed upon my back.

At one point I hovered round one of the trucks stacked with coal. It was an open-back army truck. Instead of climbing down from it to collect the next bag of coal, I just remained there, patting the bag, pretending to place it nicely among the rest. A German soldier spotted my dallying, 'Hey Jew! You're not in your shop now! Move faster!' (He was referring to the large number of shop-owners amongst Jews in prewar Europe.)

I climbed down.

The Russian POW had heard the soldier and said to me in his limited German:

'I'll put the bags on the truck, you carry.'

I was very grateful. Lifting the bags of coal into the truck was the most difficult part of the work for me.

With the very welcome help from the Russian, the bags of coal were finally reduced from a mountain to a mole-hill and then to nothing. We had finished. It was late afternoon.

Relieved, the Russian and I headed for the hospital. Walking back, the two of us said nothing. We were both indescribably tired and very dirty. Besides, he did not speak any Hungarian and only a little German, and I did not speak Russian. We were also very hungry because we had not received any food all day.

In the basement of the hospital the Russian and I washed in a small sink that we shared. I still felt so dirty. I endlessly tried to scrub the black from my face and arms. There was no soap or brush and I had to scrub with my hands until they became red. As for my clothes, there was no hope. They were black and that was that. I doubted if they could be rescued.

The hospital was run by nuns. In one area of the basement were their living quarters and in another were the boilers that heated the hospital. I finished washing and the Russian took his turn. I was ready to return back to the barracks when a nun called to me.

'Mother Superior wants to see you,' she told me.

I thought that I had unwittingly done something wrong and was in trouble. The nun took me to a door in the basement.

'This is the place,' she said and walked away.

I knocked on the door. It opened slowly and behind it stood an elderly lady.

'Hello,' she said.

She then opened the door wide. The room inside was like a seventh heaven. My eyes were wide with the miracle in front of me. A table stood in the middle of a bare room. On the table was a plain white cloth. On the cloth was a cup of coffee and two plates. One plate had sandwiches upon it and on the other were small cakes.

'You've had a hard day's work. You can't do that work on the food you get in the camp. Sit down and eat something.'

Had I really heard what the Mother Superior had just said? Was I hallucinating? I couldn't believe it! That food was for me! And what about the crockery and tablecloth! They were sights I had not seen for a long time! I was so excited. It was all so civilized, while outside barbarity raged. I headed straight for the table. All I could see was the coffee and plates of sandwiches and cakes. For me, the Mother Superior was no longer in the room. I devoured the sandwiches, thirstily drank the coffee and polished off the cakes. I felt I had achieved something. How delicious! How happy I was! I suddenly remembered the Mother Superior. She was standing a couple of metres from me! I had not noticed as my mind had been focused only on the food. I felt embarrassed at the way I must have been eating, and looked up from the table.

'Thank you very much,' I said.

The way I felt was more than words can say. I could not believe how lucky I was to be among such decent people. I left my seat and she opened the door. As the door opened, I could see the Russian POW was waiting outside. The treat was not only reserved for me. It was possible that the Russian was dealt this kindness every day. Maybe this work was not so bad after all. I would never forget this moment. The Mother Superior and her table of goodies was a light shining in the darkness of life.

The next day I had second thoughts about the trade-off between cakes, coffee and work. There was no more coal to deliver, so I went straight to the hospital. I was to shovel coal into the boilers which fed the central heating system of the hospital. It was difficult for two people to feed the boilers of a hospital, especially one that served a whole town. The Russian POW showed me what to do. We both shovelled the coal into a chute which led to the boilers. As there was a finite amount of coal every day, we tried to finish as quickly as possible so we could then relax. Naturally, it was extremely hot in there. The heat in the basement contrasted sharply with the ever colder days, but on leaving the hospital the cold air revitalized and refreshed me.

The Russian POW looked better than those I had seen working at the railway station. Their clothes were more torn and their appearance more tired. They were not protected by the Red Cross because the Soviet Union was not a member of that organization. They did not receive parcels like Allied POWs. The Russian POW was really quite well off where he was. The work was difficult but not life-threatening, and he was not seriously maltreated. Large numbers of captured Soviet troops on the Eastern Front were shot, worked to death and wholly brutalized. This Russian soldier would survive the war to return home.

Every morning at about 10.30 a nun would sweetly announce: 'Tea-time please,' and take us to that room where I had eaten the first day and where the Russian apparently ate every day. Even though I got to see this sight a second, third, fourth time, I could never believe my eyes. How could they produce this treat every day in wartime? And for a Russian POW and a Jew! The regular menu was coffee, rolls and butter cakes, but we never tired of it. How could we? There was little else for us to eat. We had a great time! Then the two of us went back to work. It was hard, but the earlier we finished, the more we could relax.

Every day for a fortnight I continued to shovel coal at the hospital. At first my hands became terribly blistered and the dirt from the work only made them worse. All I could do was to place them in water and accept the pain. The Russian told me my skin would repair itself naturally and I would become used to it as he had done. Putting bandages around my palms would be futile as they would be dirtied and quickly torn by simply picking up the shovel. However, I received a message that Schulz was well again and I was to return to work in the cemetery. For now, I left the demanding work in the hospital and those friendly and charming nuns.

8 An Unforgettable Christmas

The snow fell and Christmas approached. It was to be the last Christmas of the war. The Jewish festival that falls at this time of year, Chanukah, the festival of lights, was impossible to celebrate. All Jewish holy days and festivals were ignored by most of us. They were impossible to adhere to in such circumstances. On Saturday, the Jewish sabbath, we all had to work. Even the most fervently religious like Mr Biederman could not avoid their orders, but they would not do anything they could avoid. On the Jewish sabbath no work of any kind is allowed, including lighting a fire for a stove. The most religious of us would keep to such rules. Because one is not permitted to ask another to light a fire and so break the rules, Mr Biederman would resort to subtle tactics.

In our barn we were given a small stove for heating during the winter. Therefore, on the sabbath Mr Biederman would suddenly start discussing the weather.

'Oh, it's so cold this winter,' he would say.

He would rub his hands and arms and say to himself, 'It's so cold,' but loud enough so the rest of us could hear. I would understand and then light the stove.

All of us prayed on the sabbath (Saturday) before work, although Joe and I were not so religious and often missed Saturday prayers. The others also prayed in the morning during the week. Joe and I limited ourselves to the sabbath, but every morning my first sight of the day was Mr Biederman praying.

Occasionally, I bought a newspaper, and the most widely available was the Nazi party mouthpiece, the *Volkischer Beobachter*. I passed it amongst us and we read that the Axis forces had made a 'tactical pullback' in Budapest. We guessed this meant they had retreated and the Russians had forced them back. The Red Army was moving closer to Austria's borders. Yet again, our day of freedom which we longed for seemed to be closer.

As the cold began to bite, work in the Forstgarten became pointless. Therefore, most of the camp was sent to the *Fahrschule*, or military driving school, which was on the edge of town. It was on the opposite side of Mistelbach from the Forstgarten. In the *Fahrschule*, soldiers were taught how to drive trucks, cars, panzer wagons and all sorts of military vehicles. Joe and I joined the group. Mr Biederman, Mr Ziegelman, Mr Adler, Uncle Kiss, Sarah's mother and Joe's mother were left behind at the Forstgarten. The latter two to look after the children and the men to collect wood in the forest.

The *Fahrschule* housed about 800–1,000 soldiers. The camp was filled with trucks, armoured vehicles and a few amphibious craft. Allied bombing had caused huge oil shortages and so most of the vehicles ran on wood gas. We received pieces of wood, sliced like a cucumber, about 50 centimetres across and ten centimetres thick. We then put them flat into a machine which cut them into smaller pieces. Next we put these smaller pieces into a huge container. A truck would then come to collect the wood from the containers. The truck had a tank and into the tank we shovelled the wood using a kind of garden fork. This fork was about four times as big as a normal garden fork and not sharp. Even though the wood was light, the forks were heavy. It was hard work so we would alternate between shovelling the wood and using the machine. The trucks entered a bay and we loaded the wood into their tanks. The tanks could only be filled three-quarters full – something to do with the gas that was later produced. I never fully understood how the Germans could create gas from wood and then power vehicles from it; I was no scientist. The *holzgas* (wood gas) was an invention born of necessity.

A German sergeant gave us duties and oversaw our activities. We were forbidden to speak to any of the soldiers and they had orders to ignore us. None of us wanted to speak to the troops, and I suppose none of them had any great desire to speak to us. We had little direct contact with any of the soldiers. Our group arrived in the morning, left in the early evening and were kept to a corner of the camp. It suited us fine. However, the soldiers had been brought up to hate Jews, and it showed. Many would shout a barrage of abuse at us. They were like a bully and his gang in a school yard: full of mindless comments, nasty and spiteful. A bully is always desperately trying to hurt his prey, but deep down hides all sorts of insecurities. Perhaps one of those insecurities was the fact that the German army was being pushed back and beaten. They would yet be humbled.

However, just because many of the troops shouted abuse at us, it did not mean everyone was unpleasant. A few days after beginning work at the military camp, Valerie gashed her finger on the cutting machine. (It was a dangerous device and could easily cut a finger clean off.) She was treated by the camp doctor who was a captain in the German army. He was gentle with her and told my sister that his grandfather on his mother's side was Jewish. In Nazi ideology, seven generations had to be pure German to be free of 'polluted Jewish blood'. According to German law he was a Jew. His secret was safe with us.

The camp also housed a few Italian troops. They wore German uniforms but without German insignia. They were simply the mechanics and were signed up to work in the garages. The Italians often spoke to us, but only if none of the German troops were present. Our contact only took place at lunchtime which was 45 minutes long, beginning at midday. It was to another Italian, Philipi Netti, we went for lunch. The menu was, of course, soup. The Italian soldiers though were very civil, they sometimes gave us a little food from their own if they could spare it.

The Italian troops working in one of the garages warned me of a German captain who was their commanding officer. One of his duties was to check the running of the garage and its tidiness. I had been chosen to tidy and clean the front area of the garage. It was littered with nuts and bolts, paper, vehicle parts and all manner of things. Working alone, it took about two hours before the front area of the garage was orderly and neat in appearance. It was a huge place filled with trucks. After I had finished the captain came to inspect my work. He was power-crazy. Despite the fact he was merely one captain of thousands in the German army, he wanted everyone to know he had authority and was willing to enforce discipline even upon a harmless 15-year-old boy.

'You'd better be careful,' the Italians told me in their competent German.

'He's a bastard. If you make one mistake, I don't know what

he'll do to you,' one warned me.

'He thinks he's a general. One speck of dirt and you're in big trouble,' another said.

The Italian troops also told me how much they hated him, and that he was always looking for the tiniest mistake to pick up on so that he could use his authority.

When the captain arrived I could see why they disliked him so much. He had the most evil eyes I had ever seen. If indeed the soul of a man can be seen through his eyes, then he appeared to be one of Satan's henchmen. He looked and looked and looked: up, down, everywhere. I do not how long it lasted but it seemed an eternity. At last he looked me up and down and left without a word. I had been nervous, but besides this I thought to myself, 'Is this what I'm going to have to put up with every day from now on?'

I had to clean and tidy the front of the garage the following two days. It was the same routine from the captain and the same tenseness on my behalf each time. However, yet again Lady Luck smiled upon me. The captain went on leave and I was moved back to the wood-cutting machines. He never returned. One of the Italian troops told me that the captain had been killed in an attack on a train he had been travelling on. I cannot say that I was sorry.

The sergeant in charge of our group from the Forstgarten asked me one day to go and meet his friend, an ethnic German from Hungary, who had joined the German army. He said the man spoke Hungarian, so I could speak to someone in my own language. The sergeant also told me that he had something waiting for me. I wondered what it could be. Would a German soldier give me some food like the Italian troops had?

I went to the joinery and met the sergeant's friend, who gave me a bag. Both men apparently slept in the same living quarters.

'Look in the bag,' the joiner ordered.

I opened it and inside were tiny pieces of wood. What a disappointment! There was no food.

'Don't let the officers see you,' he warned.

I was told to take a roundabout route to his barracks where I should prepare the stove for a fire. There was paper already there to get it started.

Every day for a two-week period I went to the joinery where large pieces of plywood were cut into tiny pieces. I then took a bag full of wood and prepared a fire in the stove of their quarters for the evening. I was told what route to take to avoid any officers who might suspect what was going on. The soldiers were in effect stealing from their own stores. It was undoubtedly cold and to ensure their quarters were suitably warm they were taking wood from the army's supplies. When I prepared the stove I would try to read the newspapers to see if I could understand any of the headlines and find out about the situation in the war. If I saw an interesting article I would rip it out and put it in my pocket for my father to read, as he could understand written German well. I didn't waste too much time though, otherwise the sergeant would wonder what I was doing alone in his quarters for so long. There was nothing unusual about a Jew going to make a fire in some German troops' quarters. It would have been suspicious if I had gone once, but not every day. Nevertheless, I did have an unusual amount of wood. No one noticed however, and when the soldiers returned in the evening they had a very warm room.

Christmas Eve and Christmas Day were holidays for everyone at the Forstgarten, despite the war. On the evening of Christmas Eve I sneaked to the edge of town, as I often did, to beg for some food. The usual routine was to knock on people's doors, hoping that someone would give me food and not tell me to get lost. As it was Christmas time, I hoped that the season of goodwill to all men would also apply to me. By now the neighbours knew my face well, and they most probably knew I was Jewish. It was a small town and by day it was impossible to avoid being noticed wearing my yellow star. At the Forstgarten we had heard of a group of 21 Jews staying in the old synagogue on the other side of town, although we had not met any of them. It was a safe bet that people knew of the Jews who lived near the stream.

It was most definitely a white Christmas. Snow lay on the ground and the houses were decorated with lights. Who would have thought that a war raged? The night was still; the streets were deserted. The cold weather tested my resolve, yet I knew this was a *schnorrering* opportunity not to be missed. I knocked on a door and a man in his forties answered it.

1. Imre Schonberger wearing US Army surplus clothes a few months after the war, 1946.

2. Hauptplatz before 1900, on the east side: there was a Jewish business in the main square of the town at the turn of the century.

3. The street by the church, in 1905. Imre used to work here
in the cemetery.

4. A Nazi rally in Mistelbach during the war (c.1939).

5. The City Hall.

6. Mistelbach synagogue.

7. During the war the square in the middle of the town was renamed Hitlerplatz (Hitler Square).

8. This illustration of the hospital was specially sent to Imre by the museum, as he worked there for a number of months. The sisters were very good and helpful to him during his time there.

9. The sisters of the hospital. When working in the hospital, the nuns wore a white uniform.

10. The army camp, where Imre worked during the winter of 1944/45.

'Merry Christmas!' I said, hopefully. 'Could you spare any potatoes, please?'

'Sorry, I can't give you any, I don't have enough for myself,' he claimed.

I thought by saying 'Merry Christmas', I would get round them. However, no luck on this occasion. Continuing on to the next house, I suddenly spotted a policeman on the corner of the street. I halted, anxiously waiting to see what his reaction would be. He looked me in the eye, then turned his head, walking in the opposite direction. I was pleasantly surprised and heaved a sigh of relief. It was Christmas and the policeman was observing goodwill and peace to all men.

Just then a woman came out from a nearby house. She too was in her forties and gestured to me to approach, re-entering her house but leaving the door ajar so I could come in. I entered the house, where a man in his sixties stood in the hall. Before I could say anything, the woman popped her head from inside a room which ran off the hall and gestured to me to enter. The man remained silent.

Inside the room, a picture of a young soldier dressed in an SS uniform hung on the wall. There was black ribbon around the picture frame. I thought, 'What's going on here? Is this a trap or a black joke?' The woman began to cry.

'This is my only son,' she began to lament. 'He was here last Christmas but was killed in the Normandy invasion. He was in a supply convoy. The planes came and shot to pieces the cars, trucks, everything. He is buried in France. That was not the reason I brought him up, to join the SS and be killed.'

She then went into the kitchen. The man, who I assumed was her husband, but could have even been her father, joined me in what was a sitting room. He sat in a chair and the woman then came out from the kitchen and gave me a bag. She wiped away her tears and gestured me to leave. I walked into the hall and she opened the door to let me out. I had almost forgotten my manners in the emotion of the moment.

'Thank you very much. You're very kind. Merry Christmas.'

I left and continued on to some more houses. It was bitterly cold. I wondered if the woman had known I was Jewish. I had ventured outside my 'patch', but not too far, and covered my yellow star. However, she was no supporter of war; she had lost her only son.

I returned that evening, cold and wet. Light snow had fallen, but what I had brought would have put Santa Claus to shame. I had a bag of goodies and felt like Father Christmas with presents for all the family. It was an unforgettable Christmas. Most of us at the Forstgarten barracks had gone out to ask for food. We knew Christmas Eve was a holy night, and the people of Mistelbach might be more inclined to give on this night. My bounty included nut-cake, honey-cake and some ham, which the woman with the dead son had given to me. When I opened my rucksack my family's eyes nearly popped out. I also had cheese, more ham and bread. Everyone who had ventured out had brought back something. It was our Christmas feast. It was unbelievable, as was our joy.

On New Year's Day my Uncle Joe was caught by an SS officer with a rucksack of food he had collected from *schnorrering* in the local area. He had been struck in the face by the man and taken to the police station where the SS officer had complained that the people of the town were helping the Jews. The officer had returned to Mistelbach, his hometown, for the holidays and was leaving when he had caught my uncle. Once the SS officer had left town, the local police let Uncle Joe out of jail. He had been held only for four hours in one of the police station's cells. His rucksack was returned with the potatoes and bread he had been given still inside it.

That evening, my father and Uncle Joe sat me down and gave me some advice about my *schnorrering* activities.

'It's the holiday season; all sorts of Nazis are coming home for visits. Not everyone is a Nazi. You know that many people are willing to give us food and are decent human beings, but there are Nazis in this town too. Let's not go out in the next few days.' It was sound advice and I heeded it.

The New Year brought colder weather, and I returned to working in Frau Dunkler's construction firm. I tidied up the yard while everyone else continued to work in the military camp.

A week after my uncle had been caught by an SS officer, I was in trouble myself. So much for all that advice I had been given! I had waited hadn't I? The holiday season was over. Perhaps we had just been unlucky.

I was making my way back to the Forstgarten from Dunkler's construction yard. It was dark and I was at the edge of town. I had just knocked on a house door and asked for some potatoes. The farmer in this particular house regularly provided me with food, and I wore my yellow star without worry. I was just going out of the front gate when quite unexpectedly, someone shouted in my direction.

'Hey you! What are you doing?'

It was a member of the SS. He strode over to me. I pulled the large collar on my winter coat over my yellow star, but it was too late. Begging is frowned upon in any society no matter who does it, but no one was permitted to ask for food, especially a Jew. The SS soldier grabbed my *brotsack* and opened it. Inside were the potatoes.

'Come with me!' he screamed.

He grabbed me by my jacket and dragged me along the street, so that I could hardly walk fast enough to keep up with him. He kept a firm grip on my wrist, his hand wrapped around my arm until arriving at the town hall. This was where the offices of the police and plain-clothes police were situated.

I was taken to one of the clerk's desks and the SS soldier emptied the contents of my *brotsack* onto it. He screamed: 'Look at this! This is why the war is going badly. The people are helping those swines!' And with that he turned and stormed off.

The clerk sitting at the desk just looked at me. Then she looked to either side of her and behind her and quite matter of factly picked up the half of the sandwich she was eating and held it out in my direction. I looked in the direction of where the SS officer had gone.

'Don't worry, he won't be back yet,' she said.

I took the sandwich and stuffed it all into my mouth at once. I gulped it down and said, 'Thank you.' (Fortunately, I'd had lots of practice!)

I waited. The potatoes remained on the table. The clerk bit into an apple. It was nice to be inside. It was warm. I waited longer. I was not too worried though; the police had let my uncle go.

One hour later the police chief came to where I was sitting. He put the potatoes back into the *brotsack* and handed the lot to me.

'Get lost! I don't want to see you again!' he said curtly. The clerk showed me to the door. I was free.

I was two hours late returning to the barracks, but safe. Naturally, my family had been worried. Everyone listened as I told them of my great adventure. After this incident I was more careful. I had learned a lesson. From now on I decided to cut down on *schnorrering*. I would not go looking for food at the weekend. However, the hunt for food had to go on.

9 The Hunt and the Wait

Throughout January, I continued to go to the construction firm while everyone else visited the *Fahrschule*. We all knew that the war was going in the Allies' favour. In the *Wiener Kleine Zeitung*, a tabloid-sized Viennese newspaper, we had read that the ultra-right wing, Arrow Cross, had taken over the Hungarian government. However, Pest, the eastern side of Budapest, had fallen to the Red Army on 18 January. The person who supplied us with this newspaper was Herr Jaeger: a tall, round-faced chubby man, who was in charge of all the district's horticultural centres, like the Forstgarten. He was Brussman's boss and organized the distribution of coal to feed our small stove in the barn and milk for Joe's baby nephew. The *Wiener Kleine Zeitung* was not a Nazi mouthpiece, although all papers were censored. Between the lines we could understand what was really happening.

At the end of January, there was yet more trouble for me. It was turning into an eventful month for all the wrong reasons. I was suffering from an infection I had never seen before: a rash on both my legs with pus oozing from them. Sarah said it was due to lack of vitamins, but no more of them could be provided. She asked Jaeger to obtain some kind of cream and bandages. A few days later he returned with them. Sarah did the best she could in the circumstances. She boiled water, bathed my legs, applied cream to the wounds and bandaged them. I could walk around, but only for a few minutes. This meant I could not go to work for ten days, although Dunkler did not seem to miss me desperately. It was still very cold and there were not many jobs to do. During winter, any construction business is difficult to work on because of frost, snow and water freezing over.

With the great difficulty of keeping warm and the ever-increasing effects of poor diet, some of us at the barracks were beginning to come down with the flu – difficult to escape in winter during the best of circumstances. However, none of us ever suffered from an illness that was life-threatening and the children, including Joe's baby nephew, were sturdy characters who bore up well.

In February, Jaeger arranged for my father to go to the large hospital in Korneuburg, a suburb of Vienna. My father had suffered from a stomach ulcer for 25 years, and now he had complications. Naturally, we were all worried. Even in peacetime, when proper medical facilities were available, ulcers could kill if the complication was serious enough. My father had permanent pains in his stomach. He mentioned this to Jaeger, who organized his train ticket, his stay at the hospital and a special pass to get him to Korneuburg and back. He was to stay in the so-called 'French barracks' which was situated at the edge of the hospital. It had been named because of the large number of French POWs that had stayed there a few years before. Now it housed civilian prisoners, an assortment of POWs from various countries, and some Jews for treatment. We hoped that, despite his being Jewish, the doctors would be able to treat his ulcer to the best of their ability.

However, we soon had terrible news brought to us by Brussman. The day my father was due to be discharged, Allied aircraft had undertaken a wave of bombing against Vienna. The hospital had been hit and many killed.

'Remember,' he began, 'when a city is bombed communication stops, it doesn't mean he's dead if he isn't back from Vienna for a few days.'

But his words could not console my family and me. All of us were very anxious. My mother cried. She lamented, 'He's survived the hardship our enemies have brought us, and instead the Allies may have killed him.'

We waited. There was that kind of atmosphere when something goes dreadfully wrong and no one knows what to do or what to say.

That evening the older men discussed as usual their hopes for the future, but I was silent and Joe was too. Possibly this was some kind of emotional support. The others continued; they did not seem to think there was anything to be concerned about.

'He'll be back, don't worry,' Mr Ziegelman said. I was not so sure.

We waited. A second evening passed and he still had not

returned. By this time I was once again shovelling coal in the hospital. Those kindly nuns gave me a break from my worry, but that is all it was, a break. Even as I shovelled coal into the chute and the heat exhausted my energy, I wondered, 'Where are you Dad?'

On the third evening Joe was just arriving back from his work at a separate construction company when he saw a lonely figure in the distance, heading towards the Forstgarten. He rushed into the larger of the two barns, where I was sitting with my family and some of the others. Conversation was stilted and Joe broke the silence.

'There's someone coming here!' he exclaimed.

The comment was unusual because no one visited us at night. Only Brussman, Jaeger and Mitzi ever came to our barracks.

My mother, sisters, uncles and aunts all got up and walked outside into the dark. The figure had by now crossed the bridge. It came closer. Still only a silhouetted figure approached, ever nearer. We all waited.

'Dad!' Eva shouted.

Yes, it was my father! Our first reaction for some strange reason was not to hug or kiss, but we all applauded. A great round of applause congratulated him that he had made it back safely. Then we hugged him and kissed him. After the initial euphoria of his return, we sat down and all 27 of us listened to his story.

The hospital had been hit in the raid. Those bombs had been meant for a nearby munitions factory, but accuracy can never be guaranteed. The main building had been badly damaged and many wounded and killed. The wooden 'French barracks' had escaped being hit. My father and those others housed there had then been left wandering the streets. They had been removed from the wooden building to make way for the wounded from the main building and were left unwanted and without supervision to move freely in the aftermath. However, their free movement was based upon the anarchy that had followed the bombing. In actual fact they had been discarded, like an unwanted pet given as a present for Christmas and then thrown on the streets to roam alone. My father had been looking for food, as had the others in the aftermath. He had not eaten in three days, and the aggravation caused by the whole episode had done his ulcer no good at all. His lateness was due to the confusion following the attack – and the fact that he had had to wait until a train became available before he could return.

Now our family was reunited. We could relax a little. Some more good fortune had been bestowed upon us. I could sleep easier at night and enjoy my tea-break with the nuns in the morning.

One Sunday, Joe and I were ordered to take part in a special event, a hunt. Members of the town's elite were going hunting in the countryside. The mayor, civil servants and top consultants from the hospital would be present, although the leader of the hunt would be a young SS officer. I was rather hesitant on discovering this as my knowledge of the SS was all unsavoury to say the least.

At about ten o'clock in the morning we walked with the forest ranger to the forest. The town's elite was going hunting for rabbits. Joe and I were to act as beaters, to chase rabbits out of the undergrowth. Any running rabbits were targets. The ranger, SS officer, Joe and I, stayed 15 metres ahead of the rest of the hunting party. Shots rang out behind us in the distance. I did not know how well they were doing, but I was sure the rabbits were not enjoying themselves.

The ranger and officer kept Joe and I busy with a constant barrage of orders. We had to listen carefully and we kept changing direction. Their Austrian accents were not easy to understand. The undergrowth was thick, full of brambles and branches and difficult to pass through as quickly as they desired. It was extremely tiring on your ears, your wits and your body. At one o'clock we were able to rest and eat.

After lunch, round two began. Once again Joe and I banged and knocked the greenery of the forest to force out the terrified rabbits. However, I still could not understand properly what was being said, although Joe seemed to be coping. Unexpectedly, the SS officer stopped in his tracks and began shouting at me. He was ranting and raving. Through the barrage of abuse I could understand that I had supposedly turned left instead of right, and because of this a rabbit had escaped his bloodthirsty grasp. The ranger soothed his temper in German I could not understand and we continued forward again. Whether the forest lacked the numbers of rabbits the hunting party wished to kill or our banging and knocking did not frighten out enough rabbits from the undergrowth, both Joe and I were soon being cursed once more by the SS officer.

We approached a clearing in the forest where the hunting party planned to have tea. We were in sight of the clearing, when I turned and saw the SS officer running at me with the stick he had been using to beat the undergrowth. I took one look at the anger and hatred in his eyes and ran. I felt him close as the branches snapped underfoot, but I was faster despite my lack of nutrition and the toil of heavy work over the past months. The sound of snapping wood became more distant as I increased the gap between the two of us. Suddenly, a little way ahead of me, I noticed a clearing and could hardly believe my eyes when I saw a group of well-dressed people sitting at one of two tables in the middle of the forest! The other table was empty. Both tables were covered with a tablecloth and as I ran closer, I could see cups and saucers. It was bizarre. I entered the clearing, the SS officer still in pursuit.

'Alfred what are you doing?' I heard someone shout.

I stopped a few metres beyond the tables, exhausted, and thought perhaps this group of well-dressed individuals would prevent me from being beaten.

'Alfred what are you doing?' the voice repeated.

A woman in her late twenties stood up from her chair. The officer had now reached the clearing too. He was panting as his chase came to a halt, took a deep breath and said,

'That bastard is stupid!'

I could understand that! He had an accent but those words had been said too many times to disguise them.

I did not know or care who the woman was, but she had saved me. There were people who would have said nothing if I had been beaten. She at least had some decency.

'Come and have some tea!' she ordered.

He sat down at her table. The rest of the hunting party soon caught up with us and sat down at the second table. They drank tea and chatted while Joe and I stood next to a tree, out of harm's way.

It was a very strange sight on a cold February day. Who would have thought in this quiet clearing of a peaceful forest in this corner of Austria, that the British, American and German troops were killing and maiming each other to the west of Austria? Who would believe that Budapest, to the east, had been involved in some of the most bloodthirsty fighting of the war? Yet, it was all true. Most astonishing of all was the fact that someone had the idea to have a tea-party on a grey day, in the middle of bushes, trees and foliage and while a major conflict was in progress.

The rest of the hunt ended without further incident. That evening as I huddled under my blanket in the cold night, I thought back to the late afternoon and what I had witnessed. They had sipped their tea as their world disintegrated around them. It was pure escapism, pure fantasy. The end was only months away.

I returned to work at the *Fahrschule* after a second stint at the hospital. It was easier now the bitter winter had gone. The New Year had brought leave for the Italian soldiers, but some of them had not returned. They had no more wish to be part of the German armed forces and had simply vanished. There was not much love lost between them and the German army they worked for.

Our group of 27 Jews had been joined by the 21 Jews we had heard about staying in the old Mistelbach synagogue. However, our group and theirs were kept separate, so they were merely faces in the distance.

A date imprinted on my memory was 1 March. Every day the air raid sirens sounded like clockwork between 11.30 a.m. and midday. You could set your watch by it. The Allied planes would buzz overhead and make their way to their targets. When the air raid sirens sounded, all of our group from the Forstgarten were permitted to leave the military camp to escape the danger. The German troops, because they had to stay by their posts, envied us. Their feelings of jealousy would be translated into ever more vitriolic outbursts of verbal abuse.

On 1 March the planes came early. It was between 9 and 9.30 a.m. This time there were far more planes than I had ever seen before. German fighters came to meet them. It was a deadly rendezvous. A low-flying fighter suddenly dived from the mass of metal above in the direction of the *Fahrschule*. It was the first time

we had come under attack. There was no time to escape.
Soldiers screamed,

'Get on the ground!'

Machine gun-fire opened up on the plane as it dived.
Everyone hit the ground, but in panic, one person from the
group of Jews staying in the synagogue dived under an oil
tanker. (Luckily it was empty and the middle-aged gentleman
lived to tell the tale.)

I continued to visit the shops. On one occasion I asked the shopkeeper for anything she could sell me that did not need ration
coupons. She told me that the only thing she could spare was
Kunsthonig – artificial honey. It was white and syrup-like and
came in a small cardboard container. It did not taste like honey,
but was very sweet. I shared it as usual amongst my immediate
family and we spread it on bread.

A familiar sight as I walked into town that I saw on shop
walls, doors, in the train station, public buildings, almost everywhere, was one particular poster that stood out in my memory.
It was a picture of a man dressed in a long black coat and black
hat, with his hand to his ear, slightly leaning forward, as if listening to something. Along the bottom was written, *'Achtung!
Der Feind Hort Mit.'* [Watch out! The enemy is listening.]

Sunday was usually a rest day. Joe and I would take milk cans
to Philipi Netti's restaurant to collect food, as we had done on
the very first day in Mistelbach. One Sunday afternoon, Netti
asked us to wait for 20 minutes. He was very friendly and in a
good mood, and he gave us both some meat. (He had done that
only once before, on our first day in Mistelbach.)

'I'm going to teach you how to kill rats,' he said knowingly.

In his hands he held a pellet rifle. He took us both to a large
wine cellar in the basement of the restaurant. The walls had a
number of holes in them and this was where he told us the rats
lived. He placed sticks of phosphor at the mouths of the holes
and lit them. The rats, dazed, stumbled out of the holes. Netti
then shot them one by one, killing about 15. I think he wanted
to show us what a good marksman he was, despite the fact the
rats were barely moving targets. It was an education all the
same, but I wanted to say to him, 'Could you hurry up please,
the food is getting cold.'

10 Goodbye Mistelbach

The war now encroached upon us every day; it was inescapable. Night after night we heard rumbling noises in the distance. My father said it was artillery fire. Whatever it was, it was relentless.

Soon we heard that the Russian army had completely surrounded Vienna. Mistelbach was just 45 kilometres from the Austrian capital. We were both frightened and excited at the prospect of the Red Army's approach. The roar of their fighting machine scared us at night, but their advance gave us further cause for hope.

On 5 April, I was working in the hospital and receiving the regular morning coffee and snacks. At the end of the day the Mother Superior unusually asked me to see her in the late afternoon.

'Thank you for your work but I won't be seeing you tomorrow,' she told me. 'You won't be coming to work at the hospital again. Good luck.'

I was startled and surprised. That was odd. Just like that I was being told I was not coming to the hospital again, and by the Mother Superior. Normally Dunkler or Brussman told me which day I was going to work, for whom and normally in advance.

I asked the Mother Superior, 'Where will I be going to tomorrow?'

'I don't know,' she replied, but I was not so sure.

As I walked back to the Forstgarten I wondered what I would be doing the following day and what really was happening. It was all very odd, very strange.

Maybe the answer lay in my subsequent encounter.

I knocked on the door of a farmer, whose house was situated not far from the Forstgarten. I was intending to ask for potatoes or bread, as I usually did. On this occasion I was invited by the farmer to enter his home and speak with his family. It seemed my day was becoming increasingly unusual. The farmer showed me into the sitting room where he told me they were just finishing their meal.

A young man dressed in an SS uniform was sitting at the table. My first thought was that the farmer had handed me over to the SS. The youth appeared to be about seventeen and was slim with short blonde hair. I looked at him with apprehension. It must have shown in my eyes.

'Don't worry,' he started the conversation, 'the war will be over soon. The Russians took Malacki the other day. It's a Czech town on the Austrian border.'

I thought this whole incident was some black comedy. A farmer had asked me to enter his home, where a youth dressed in a uniform told me to 'not to worry' because the war would be over soon. Was I dreaming? Yet there was more to come.

The young man then handed me the latest leaflet of the *Rot—Weiss–Rot*, the London-edited Austrian emigré paper, dropped by planes. An SS soldier handing a Jew 'enemy' material!

'This is my son,' the farmer said.

'My wife will give you some potatoes,' he told me.

His wife, indifferent to my presence then entered the sitting room from the kitchen. She too must have been able to read the anxiety written all over my face.

'My son is wearing an SS uniform, but he is not SS,' she claimed and then turned to her son and said, 'Tell him,' entering the kitchen once more.

'I'm not the SS you're thinking of,' he explained. 'Some soldiers came to Mistelbach. I was in high school. They took the boys out in the yard and told us that the armed forces have had heavy losses. Then they said "You over there, Wermacht, you over there SS" and divided us up like that. We weren't volunteers.'

The wife who seemed eager to inform me her son was not an SS volunteer then came back into the sitting room with some potatoes in her hands. I opened my *brotsack* and she bundled them in. I was grateful for the food and the fact that the young man whose presence I was in was not one of those volunteers. Nevertheless, I hoped he and his family were telling the truth.

I thanked the farmer, his wife and son and said goodbye. A few minutes from their home, in the clear countryside, I eagerly began to read the paper I had been given. The headlines pronounced, 'Fighting near Berlin'. The Red Army had reached the outskirts of Berlin. It was great news. The capital was bombarded day after day, and the creators of the blitzkreig were being given more than their own medicine. The paper also showed a picture of an American tank rolling into Aachen, the first occupied city in Germany. It was pleasing to say the least.

When I arrived back I showed everyone the good news. It had been a strange day with surprising events, but life was looking ever slightly rosier. That night in the barn we discussed our hopes once more.

'The Russians are giving those bastards justice,' Mr Biederman exclaimed. He continued, 'I hope I survive. I pray to G-d to survive and if I do I'm not going to save any more money. I'm going to eat the best food and make up for what I've missed.' (Mr Biederman had a grown-up son who had gone to America before the war had begun. He said he would join him if G-d let him live and his wife, the world's best cook, would, G-d willing, accompany him.)

'My son will go back to study as a doctor,' Mr Adler told us all. Nonetheless, he did not know if his son, three daughters and wife were alive. By telling us his son would return to his medical studies, he was trying to will him into being alive. As yet, he did not know of his family's fate.

Mr Ziegelman dreamt of marrying off his three daughters. He had married late, in his forties.

'I want to give them a little *nedan*,' he told us.

'You don't have to worry yet,' I insisted.

His eldest daughter was 20 years old and his youngest 16. A *nedan*, or dowry, seemed a little early yet.

'My little one is the prettiest,' he said, referring to his youngest daughter.

The mood was upbeat that evening, but the following day we all had a rude awakening. Brussman arrived very early with a man from the town hall. We were all woken and assembled at approximately 6.00 a.m., an hour before we usually rose for our daily duties.

'You won't be going to work anymore,' the man from the

town hall informed us.

'The town has become a military zone. Pack and be ready to leave tomorrow. You will join the other Jews from the synagogue. All of you will leave together from the advancing Russians.'

We were all puzzled and quiet.

'You'll be fed while travelling,' he continued, 'and you'll have some Volkssturm guards to accompany you all.'

What were we to think? Was this good news or bad news? Our reaction was to look at each other in bewilderment. Were we being moved for our own safety or to another camp? A worse camp? By becoming a military zone, Mistelbach was therefore less than 30 kilometres away from the front line. There would be no air raid warning. Everyone would have to assume a constant state of alert. An attack of any kind, artillery or from the air, was now a threat everyone had to be aware of at all times.

We returned to our thin-walled barns that had housed us for the last months to pack our belongings. Those handful of plates which my family had brought and used in the Szeged transit camp now seemed very silly items to have brought after all we had been through. They had been useful in that brick factory, but none of them had survived. Only our clothes and blankets remained. At least we had them. They had saved us during the winter.

Joe and I were told to go to Philipi Netti's restaurant and bring back some food. As usual we took large milk-cans and on entering town, the sound of artillery guns pounding Vienna suddenly became audible. In the distance we could both see dozens of civilians digging tank-traps and trenches in preparation for the defence of the town. Unexpectedly, two planes buzzed above us. Joe and I looked up and without a word ran to the nearest ditch and dived into it. Other civilians on the street also ran for cover. It was a false alarm. The planes only buzzed and flew off.

As we approached Netti's restaurant, we could see him fill milk-cans with soup and meat for men dressed in SS uniforms. He was being very polite. I was not exactly sure of Netti's role in the scheme of things but he seemed to be feeding lots of people: from the SS ready to defend the town to the Jewish workers who were about to leave it.

After Netti had filled our milk-cans with soup, Joe and I left his restaurant for the last time. The Italian restaurant owner was in a better mood than usual. I did not know why. Maybe it was all an act for the SS soldiers. But just where did he get all his food?

The milk-cans seemed heavier than usual. (Joe thought so too.) Netti had not given us any more soup than usual. Maybe our mental tiredness was affecting our physical strength, but on second thoughts, that had been long affected by our lack of vitamins, iron, minerals and everything else that goes with normal eating habits. These had been impossible for all 27 of us at the barracks for a long time.

The two of us passed the last house in Mistelbach and trudged along the single road which eventually led to the bridge that crossed the stream. I then noticed two planes in the spring sky above. Just specks in the distance, they quickly became visible flying killing machines: iron birds ready to swoop on their prey below. Joe and I were sitting ducks in the open.

'They're coming closer,' I said to Joe, 'let's run!'

He did not question me, and we put down the milk-cans just before the bridge. We ran for our lives into the forest. The planes swooped down and sprayed the road with bullets. Out of breath, we panted as we waited in the undergrowth, keeping still and silent. The buzzing sound of the planes became distant. The two of us slowly crept out from our hiding place amongst the trees. The planes were now black dots on a blue background, then they disappeared altogether. Joe saw it first. The planes had riddled the milk-cans with bullets and the soup – our only food of the day, apart from the bread and coffee for breakfast – had leaked out all over the ground. We resigned ourselves to the fact that that night everyone at the barracks would now go hungry.

Joe and I crossed the bridge. If the cans had been heavy then we had been relieved of the weight, but now no one would be fed until the next morning. Somehow we thought that between us we had let everyone else down. Our empty, holey milk-cans were met with shock and disappointment. The only good thing was that Joe and I had escaped unscathed.

That last night at the barracks all of us had only one thing on our minds – food. Everyone except the two youngest children and

Sarah, her brother and mother, swarmed on the nearby farmers' houses like locusts, trying to obtain whatever we could. (We had no idea of when our next meal would come.) For all of us it was our last great night of *schnorrering*. We packed our clothes, blankets and food. Everyone planned to wear more than one layer of clothing as our luggage space was being taken up by potatoes, bread, apples and the like. It was cool anyway, so in a manner of speaking we could kill two birds with one stone. The luggage packed, we went to sleep without talking, perhaps partly due to our activities that evening and partly because of the uncertain future that awaited us.

Only 24 people would be leaving in the morning. Sarah and her mother and brother were remaining behind in the barracks. She had been asked to serve as a doctor in the town hospital. The Third Reich, of which Austria was a part, was now so short of trained medical staff, it had resorted to requesting 'racially inferior Jews'. Sarah, not knowing where we would all be going and guaranteed of good treatment in return for remaining, had agreed. Her elderly mother would not have to march an unspecified amount of kilometres, and her brother could stay too.

The following morning Brussman, Mitzi and five members of the Volkssturm waited to escort 24 of us from the Forstgarten. I was not sorry to leave those barns. They had been dreadfully cold in the winter. In the spring and summer they were full of insects which bit you while you slept. Yet there was a kind of certainty in staying there. We would get up, eat a little food, go to work, have a little more food for lunch and finish work. We would then talk and go to bed. Now there was no such routine, only doubt. There was nothingness.

The 24 of us trudged out of the Forstgarten, and our faces expressed worry rather than happiness. No one looked back. There was no nostalgia, only another journey to our umpteenth new destination in the last 13 months. Brussman and Mitzi bade us a businesslike farewell.

We were now in the hands of the Volkssturm leader, Herr Schmidt. He was a discharged lieutenant from the German armed forces. Schmidt had been fighting on the Eastern Front and had been injured in the left leg. Consequently, he walked with a limp. In his mid thirties, of average height and with brown hair, he carried a pistol and rode a bicycle. He rarely stood. His injury was such that sitting and pedalling a bicycle was easier than standing on his two legs. I had no idea about the kind of injury that would cause such a condition. No one knew what were his orders, where he would take us or where we would sleep. The four other Volkssturm members were probably in their sixties. They carried old rifles and sticks.

We made our way across the bridge and along the road that led to town. No one said a word. It was sunny and pleasant weather. We had arrived on a June day in sunshine and we were leaving in sunshine. The countryside was once more green and in full bloom.

I soon discovered that to lift an item of luggage and to carry it for a period of time were two completely different things. My two very full bags were soon too much for me to carry. I was also wearing three layers of clothes, and they drained me more by making me hot. We had reached Main Street and I put down my bags to take a quick rest. I looked up and saw number 13 on one of the houses – unlucky perhaps. We were already attracting attention as some townspeople stopped to watch our slow movement or peered through windows. It was then that number 13 Main Street became the point where another act of human decency took place which is engraved in my memory. A white- haired old woman in her mid seventies brought out from her house a wheelbarrow. As I stood, tired, in the street and the others slowly moved on she said, 'Here son, take this. It's easier.'

The wheelbarrow had a belt which you could put over both your shoulders and so lessen the strain on your hands.

'It's much easier this way, thank you,' I told her.

'Maria, I haven't seen you for a long time,' said one of the Volkssturm to the old woman. In response she waved at him. I could not believe it. Yet, there was another surprise. The Volkssturm guard then walked over to me, I assumed, to take the wheelbarrow away from me.

'It is easier isn't it,' the man said, and winked.

I put my bags into it and took a bag each from my father, mother and sisters.

Schmidt took us to Mistelbach's only synagogue. There, at last, we met the 21 Jews who had been living in it. We had heard

about them, then seen them, now we were face to face.
Everyone made small talk. They were from the northeast of
Hungary, mostly from a city called Debrecen and its surrounding area. They had come to Mistelbach in August and consisted
of families too.

After allowing us some time to talk, Schmidt told us we had
to make our way to the nearby village of Laa, several kilometres
from Mistelbach, and it was there we now headed. Our wan-
derings in Nieder Österreich, the Austrian Lowlands, were
about to begin.

11 Wandering through Nieder Österreich

Schmidt led us along small roads. The Austrian Lowlands were comprised mainly of farms and villages. It was a sunny April in 1945. With our baggage, family and friends, we made our way slowly through beautiful scenery. Meanwhile, amongst nature's serenity, mankind was killing itself with its machines of metal. The Western Allied armies were cutting through the Ruhr in the west, and the Red Army had reached the outskirts of Berlin in the east. The local Austrians knew that the war was lost.

Schmidt cycled ahead of the group and spoke to the head man in the first village where we were to stay, Laa. It was a pattern that would be repeated time and again. Our sleeping arrangements and food were organized in advance. In this first village, as in subsequent ones, all 45 of us slept in a barn, but of course this was something we were used to. Schmidt and the other four guards from the Volkssturm slept in a farmer's house – the beginning of another regular routine.

That first night on the road, our menu was boiled potatoes and soup. This was to become a regular diet. Sometimes we might receive bread and fruit or raw potatoes to roast on an open fire. Our bed was a pile of hay together with our own blankets to keep us warm. The Volkssturm guards, sleeping in the farmer's house, did not really care if we escaped. They would not have been able to prevent us from doing so, had we wished to, but there was nowhere to go. So as yet, no one thought of escaping. The advancing Red Army was behind us and the retreating German army in front of us. We certainly could not go forward, so what about going backwards? Heading towards heavy fighting was not an option either. What about hiding in a village somewhere in the middle? How long though until the Red Army came? By having Schmidt and the Volkssturm with us, we were all guaranteed a building to sleep in, despite it only being a barn. We had the added bonus of our meals being organized for us, frugal as they were. Food and shelter was so little for anyone to ask for in peacetime, but this was wartime and these necessities could not always be secured. In addition to this, my parents knew we were fortunate – a word which would stay in our collective memory forever. They knew of Auschwitz and had been told by Sarah of the rumours in her camp before arriving at Mistelbach. Obviously my parents had no thought of telling my sisters and I. They also did not contemplate escaping. Maybe we were like so many other Jews: telling ourselves everything would be fine, but not realizing what our fate was and waiting until it was too late.

There was also a sense of security in being part of a group of 45. What would happen if my family or anyone else's had escaped? What would retreating German soldiers do to them, or a local Austrian Nazi, all disgruntled with defeat? While we waited for our Slavic rescuers, my father, a decorated soldier himself, knew only too well how some troops treated women. It was a part of warfare that was sadly ingrained in both victory and defeat since the beginning of recorded history.

We slept our first night outside Mistelbach for many months once again guessing and hoping. Our assumption was that if those Volkssturm guards did not care that we escaped, wherever they were taking us, it was not to be murdered.

A pattern emerged. By day we walked along the quietest and loneliest roads. By night we rested and ate ravenously our only meal of the day. Then we would sleep and talk. We talked while walking; we talked before sleeping. Each time Schmidt would cycle ahead to organize food and usually a barn for sleeping. Each time we were not watched over and could have escaped, if anyone had wished to.

Our talk by day and night was of what each of us would do when we were free once more. Everyone naturally hoped for a better life than before March 1944, but many wanted revenge. I never said to anyone that I wanted to see blood, but inside I wanted justice. When I was to discover what else had happened, then I would want blood!

The days passed slowly, as did the lonely roads and villages. We walked around ten to 15 kilometres a day. Mr Biederman was a good strong walker, despite being the oldest amongst us.

But someone would naturally say: 'Herr Schmidt can we rest, the children are tired,' and he would reply, 'At the next village.'

One little town we stayed at was called Ernstbrunn, a neat little town with a population of mostly farming people. The town was quiet and life appeared normal, despite the presence of soldiers. In this town we were untypically placed in a disused building. My little sister hurt her ankle, but one of the Volkssturm, who had served in the Austrian army medical core, fixed it. Schmidt had some good news for us in Ernstbrunn. The Red Army had taken Vienna and there was heavy fighting in Berlin. We knew the war would be over soon.

Schmidt claimed to be no big fan of the Nazi regime. He told someone among us that his father had been a union leader and had been arrested by the Nazi government after Austria's union with Germany in 1938. He had been interned for six months. This rumour spread amongst all of us. Yet, where he was leading us, and to what fate, we still did not know. In addition to this I wondered if Schmidt was telling us of his 'liberal' credentials because he was leading a rag-bag bunch of Jews around the Austrian lowlands at the end of the war, with the Axis powers defeat inevitable. Would he have been so forthcoming if this had been 1941? (This had been the year in which the Nazi Reich was at its height.) Then again, perhaps he did possess some liberal tendencies after all. How could we know? My family and I had seen various extremes of human nature since being forcibly deported from our home.

Our next stop was a town called Hollabrunn. It was the largest town we had seen since leaving Mistelbach. Schmidt led us into the heart of it, when we reached the main square, and saw scores of wounded soldiers and huge numbers of trucks and troops. The front line was now uncomfortably near. In the middle of the square there stood a few military police organizing the flow of traffic. I could see many injured soldiers, some with bandaged heads, others with bandaged arms or legs. It was a sight of an army in retreat and near defeat. One of the military police suddenly noticed in the midst of all this, five Volkssturm leading a group of ragged-looking Jews, all conspicuous by their yellow stars. I looked around me observing the chaos and thought to myself, 'The roads were choked enough without us being here.' The military police must have read my thoughts and one of them shouted: 'Get those Jews the hell out of this town! We've got enough people to take care of! Take them anywhere!'

The message had been clearly directed at Schmidt. We retraced our steps and headed to the nearest village. Why he had taken the route to Hollabrunn we did not know. It would be reasonable to assume he did not realize he was taking us into a mêlée of retreating troops.

Our next village, Raabs, had a beautiful flowing river by which a castle stood. It was the quietest place on our journey. The 50 of us must have seemed an odd lot to the locals, whom we seemed to outnumber. Some just stopped in the street and stared in amazement at us. And what a sight we were: unwashed for days, carrying all sorts of baggage, tired and hungry and led by four old men and a younger one on a bicycle.

At the next village something significant happened. Reinitz escaped. He had told the rest of the men from Soltvadkert, and me as well, that he did not like the uncertainty of not knowing where we were heading or what would happen to us, and he wanted to be sure of survival. For him that certainty could be guaranteed by himself, and he simply dropped out of the group before nightfall. As we settled down in an open field – our bed for the night – a middle-aged man from the group of Jews who had been resident in Mistelbach synagogue also fled. It put ideas into my teenage and impressionable head.

That evening I sat down with all my family, immediate and extended, and we discussed the recent events. I too wanted to escape.

'We don't know what will happen to us. If you want to escape you can disappear into a village, if that's what you really want,' my mother said.

'Your German isn't as good as Reinitz's,' Uncle Joe warned me.

'If you want to go I won't hold you back. We'll push the wheelbarrow, but in my experience of life I think Schmidt is a decent man,' my father surmised. He continued, 'The war will be over in a few days or at worst a couple of weeks. We've stayed together through the bad times, and we should continue to stay together until they are over.'

I was quiet, almost ashamed. My father had given the kind of speech that made me feel I was letting everyone down. My uncle made me feel as if I did not know what I was doing. My mother was undecided, perhaps thinking that if Schmidt was indeed taking us to our deaths, at least one of us would survive.

I decided to stay, consoling myself with the thought that there was safety in numbers. All the remaining 43 prisoners slept out in the open. The Volkssturm had taken refuge from the elements in a local's house. The night air seemed to test my resolve, as frost crept across the countryside and we huddled under our blankets trying to keep warm. I wondered where Reinitz was and whether some friendly locals had taken him under their wing and let him sleep in the warmth or had given him food. Then I heard a voice in my head. Maybe some local had killed him or retreating troops had abused him. There were any number of possibilities. It was not pessimistic thinking; it was reality.

Schmidt continued leading us west until reaching Horn. By now, we had been travelling for more than two weeks. He then changed direction and began taking us north towards the Czech border. Suddenly we had to make a U-turn. How he discovered we do not know, but he claimed that SS troops were retreating and that they were heading in our direction. We had to move fast. Beginning at seven in the morning, we travelled between 50 and 60 kilometres until ten o'clock that night. We stopped only a few times on the way to rest. Everyone, including the children and the elderly, despite having eaten so little, managed somehow to keep going. The spectre of SS troops in our path, true or not, made us travel an almost impossible number of kilometres in one day. (The Volkssturm themselves had barely been able to keep up.) During this trek, another man from the group of Jews formerly resident in Mistelbach synagogue also vanished. Yet again, Schmidt and the other guards did not bat an eyelid. The going was now extremely tough.

The following morning we rose early and were told to make haste. By midday, many were at the point of collapse. Schmidt had taken us on a roundabout route to reach the presumed goal – a border post overlooking Czechoslovakia. We arrived in the afternoon and were very glad of it. (In actual fact it had been a

Czech border post before the war.) We now knew that Schmidt was delivering us to the Red Army and not the agents of murder. His claim that the SS were retreating and we must avoid them was believable. He had put us through hell and everybody was absolutely exhausted, but we were at the Czech border. The armed forces of the Soviet Union could not be far away.

Schmidt led us to a very large abandoned building. It was set in beautiful countryside surrounded by open fields and was where the customs guards and border guards used to live. It had one floor, several rooms and a coal cellar.

Two of the rooms were quickly occupied. There was much puffing of cheeks and sighs as we settled down for the evening. Blankets were spread across the floor and people made their groups sit and talk.

Just as we were beginning to relax for the first time in days, a frightening sound destroyed the moment. Army trucks, light tanks and troop carriers pulled up outside the house. We stopped talking and listened intently.

'Germans!' a voice shouted suddenly breaking the silence.

Troops then poured through the front door. They were from an SS panzer division, recognizable by their black uniforms and skull on their caps. The troops walked into the room where we were encamped and were clearly surprised to see us. Schmidt moved forward to meet their commanding officer. They spoke for a couple of minutes and then the commanding officer, a tall and youthful-looking major, spoke to us all:

'I don't care who you are, but we are hungry. We want the women to cook stew for us. We have plenty of meat, potatoes and cooking oil. What is left over we will give to you.'

The soldiers brought in sacks of potatoes and several women and men, including myself, began peeling them. My mum and four other women began to make goulash. The building had two large cauldrons in the coal cellar and they were exactly what we needed to feed the 50 or so troops. My mum lit the fires beneath the cauldrons. The building was fully equipped. There was running water, wood for the fire, cooking utensils, and even spices, pepper and salt, just waiting to be used. The troops had their own military plates to eat from, which suited us because we did not possess enough for them to use.

The soldiers appeared tired and hungry, and most looked to be not much older than 20. They eagerly ate their stew in the coal cellar, their appetites unaffected by the dark and dirty surroundings. Those people who were not helping in the preparation of the food remained upstairs. My mother asked the major if the food was tasty. He told her, 'We haven't eaten such a good meal for a long time.'

All the troops seemed satisfied. Everyone wanted a second helping and the women served them again. One soldier complained, 'Where's the meat?'

My mother replied: 'There's no more, see for yourself,' and handed the soldier the huge ladle. He fished in both the cauldrons for some meat but there were only potatoes and goulash soup left.

After finishing their meal the soldiers went outside to their vehicles. Not one of them said a bad word to us. They had eaten and chatted amongst themselves. One of the women who had helped prepare the meal then called everyone else who had stayed above on the ground floor. The rest, like vultures around a half-eaten carcass, ate the remaining potatoes and goulash soup. The troop's food had served around a hundred people.

It was about 2.00 a.m. before everything had been eaten, cleaned and tidied. Everyone made their way to the ground floor and lay down uneasily with their blankets for warmth, while the troops remained outside preparing for something. One woman, sleeping close to my father, became suddenly panic-stricken.

'They're going to kill us,' she said.

'You stupid woman!' my father said scornfully, 'Don't start spreading rumours or frightening people! Let them sleep. If they wanted to kill us they would have done it by now. Go to sleep!'

I overheard this conversation, lay down and closed my eyes, but did not want to sleep, although my exhaustion overcame me. My subconscious woke me a couple of hours later. I stood up and crept over to the window, peering into the night. The troops had gone. They had been preparing to leave and not to kill. Now I could sleep easier.

Everyone slept late that following morning, all in desperate need of a good night's sleep. Taking advantage of our freedom, we rested all day, strolling near the border post, the beauty of the surrounding countryside easing our souls.

We stayed in that big empty building for a few days. The soldiers had left some potatoes behind, and somehow 42 prisoners survived on them. However, we received only the most miniscule ration each and had to manage; there was no other choice. At least we all had running water. Meanwhile, Schmidt cycled to a nearby village and brought food for the other Volkssturm.

Mr Biederman, Mr Ziegelman, Mr Adler and Uncle Kiss were bearing up well. They were tough nuts and were determined not to crack. They had 'I'm going to prove you wrong!' written all over their faces and were doing admirably. The children were looking increasingly skinny and weak, especially my younger sister. Joe, who never complained, had a baby nephew who seemed to be in fair condition, but his sister had given any food she had to her son and her cheek-bones were beginning to show through her skin. The rest of my family appeared to be fine in the circumstances. We were very hungry, but at least we had water.

Schmidt filled his empty days by occasionally leaving the border post and going off to scout. The prisoners he left behind just sat round, wandered outside or tried to think how to divide some potatoes amongst 42 people for a number of days. The other Volkssturm guards occasionally spoke with us, but mostly kept to themselves. They had done so for most of the journey and appeared to prefer matters that way. Schmidt returned from a village with food for them, eating away from us – no doubt too ashamed of their ration in comparison to ours. But it all seemed so peculiar. The Volkssturm acted as if they would rather have been anywhere else than at a border post with 42 ragged and hungry Jews. I thought that to them we appeared an encumbrance rather than an ideological kill on behalf of the Nazi state.

One day Schmidt returned with some bread. Seeing it was the equivalent of finding an oasis in a desert. We ravenously ate our ration and then he told us some fantastic news. He had heard on the radio that Hitler was dead and that Admiral Donitz was the new German head of state. There was heavy street-fighting in Berlin. It was joyful news, but difficult to take in. The Red Army in Berlin? Hitler dead? It was astounding! We all knew the war was near its end and victory for the Allies only a matter of time, but once we were told the news it seemed difficult to digest. All this wandering and living off food which would have kept a chicken hungry would actually be over soon. The news was greeted with amazement and everyone began to embrace one another with joy and relief. The war was finally over. Our war would soon be over too.

Eventually Schmidt told us it was time to move on, so we packed our belongings, reinvigorated by the news. He had brought raw potatoes over the previous two days and had told us we must keep them for our next part of the journey, which would begin soon. Schmidt had planned ahead, but we looked longingly at those potatoes on their arrival. Even one potato each would probably only last for two occasions. We had to have discipline; the food was needed for travelling.

The first week of May had brought us new hope to cling onto. It could give us the mental energy to overcome our poor physical condition. Everyone knew that if we all could hold on a little longer and not lose our heads, then our next meal was round the corner.

We took the road towards our umpteenth village, along the Austrian–Czech border. Schmidt led us to a school, arriving at about 11.00 a.m. It was comfortable and clean. My mother said what luck it was that we could stay in such a nice place. We sat down and waited. However, our joy was short lived for at 3.00 p.m. the order came to leave the town. It was crowded with the retreating German army which wanted the school for its troops.

We gathered up our belongings and meagre food supplies and walked a further ten kilometres to a nearby town. It was a farming area full of retreating panzer units. It seemed that we had jumped from the frying pan into the fire. We made our way to the town square, arriving in the evening. Schmidt told us to wait while he looked for somewhere to sleep. It was a warm evening and we all sat down in the square, just in sight of retreating German troops with military vehicles.

Suddenly, rockets known as Stalin candles began to fall. I noted more than 30 before losing count. The whole square was lit up in a matter of minutes. It was so light that you could read a newspaper. The German soldiers were running for cover. They camouflaged their vehicles and fled. We were now sitting-ducks for any bombs Allied aircraft wished to throw at us. Everyone was frozen with fear to the ground they sat on. Uncle Kiss stood up.

'Please Lord, just one more time, please let me live, please give us one more chance to survive the war,' and he looked upwards to the illuminated sky above and prayed for a miracle.

'Get the hell out of here!' a German soldier shouted.

Everybody simultaneously stood up and ran for their lives into the nearby streets.

The roar of Allied aircraft frightened everyone even more. Mr Biederman had been saying evening prayers by a house on the corner of the square. He did not flinch and continued. One German soldier screamed: 'You old idiot! Run if you want to live!'

Mr Biederman turned his head in the direction of the voice and then continued with his prayers. He was just reaching the end of the Amidah, a Jewish prayer which one is forbidden to interrupt. As I lay down on the ground I could see he was determined to finish it.

I watched him pray and thought back to Jewish school where I had learnt about King David and how he had been studying on the sabbath to avoid dying. Was Mr Biederman doing something similar? Were his faith and belief so strong? Or was he indeed just an old idiot?

It took him a minute or so to finish and then, as if his stubborn reaction had not taken place at all, he collapsed onto the ground with his hands over his head.

For ten minutes everyone lay on the earth and prayed. Minutes seemed like hours. The planes hovered overhead and we waited for the bombs to fall. However, slowly the lights of the rockets faded, one by one by one. Darkness fell again. The aircraft flew away. We summoned up the courage to stand up and return to the square.

The old men's prayers were answered. The Stalin candles had burnt out and the bombs never fell. The aircraft did not find what they were looking for and flew away. The German troops had been relatively quick in camouflaging their vehicles. Everyone genuinely thanked G-d for saving us.

Schmidt led us to a barn and we slept soundly, despite the earlier events. The straw seemed comforting until we were rudely woken by anti-aircraft fire in the distance. Nobody could sleep now, only sigh.

Early next morning, Schmidt persuaded a local farmer to bring the children milk. The farmers could not transport or sell it because of the increasingly anarchic situation, so they gave it away.

Another farmer brought us potatoes which we cooked on an open fire. The atmosphere was very optimistic despite the previous night's events. We felt we had been through our last danger. The storm had been weathered and blue skies lay ahead. Everyone seemed to have had a weight taken off their minds and appeared relaxed.

We remained in this town for another night without incident. The farmers brought us milk again for the children and potatoes for all of us. We made our way to the next village, the final stage on our epic tour of Austria's countryside.

Schmidt led us once again to a barn. It belonged to a small farm and had a large yard adjacent to it. It was midday and the Volkssturm leader asked the farmer to provide us all with soup, which he dutifully did, little as it was. After eating, Schmidt had some surprising news.

He asked to speak to my father and three other men from the group of Jews who had been resident in Mistelbach synagogue. Schmidt told them that he and the other Volkssturm were leaving. He then gave some useful advice. As few people as possible should be allowed to go into the village to obtain food, especially the old men with long beards. In addition, it would be better to remove our yellow stars. Any retreating ill-disciplined soldiers might take a pot shot at a Jew and not think twice about doing so. The utmost caution was called for. Officially we were the responsibility of the village head. All five Volkssturm shook hands with my dad and the other three and quietly made their exit.

Everyone looked on as the Volkssturm left, and we all must have wondered where all five were going. My father told us all of the new developments. The reaction was of pleasant surprise, but at the same time worry about our immediate future. Perhaps

94

everyone had pictures in their minds of marauding soldiers searching for Jews to shoot. Of course, no comments about keeping long-bearded Jews off the streets were made, but everyone received the message loud and clear not to go wandering away by themselves just because the Volkssturm had left.

After my father had finished his message, my first reaction was to rip off the yellow star which had been attached to my clothing for so long. Everyone seemed to have a similar thought going through their minds and quickly followed suit. It was 4 May. I could not remember every date on which an incident had happened since leaving Mistelbach. I could not remember every town's name I had been to since leaving there. However, I could remember 4 May 1945, the day I was at last free of that yellow star. It had taken more than a year, but that symbol of exaggerated division had gone.

We remained quietly in the area of the barn and yard. In the evening, the major topic of conversation was who would arrive first in this village to 'officially' liberate us: the Americans or the Russians. Schmidt had told us the Americans had taken Linz, but we did not know if they were advancing further.

The following day I ventured into the village to look for food. The farmer whose barn we were staying in kindly gave us some potatoes in the morning. (It seemed there was a never-ending supply of them, for which we were truly grateful.) While enjoying my new freedom in the village, I stopped outside a butcher's shop. The owner, a short stocky man, called me in.

'Hey, come here!' he shouted.

'What part would you like?' he asked, gesturing at a pig hanging on a hook.

I pointed at the leg and he took his knife and cut a large piece of ham from the top of it. I was so pleased that I did not venture any further into the village and rushed back to show my prize to my family. It was shared amongst them and we ate it with some potatoes, cooked once again over an open fire in a small corner of the yard. It would have been wonderful to share any food we obtained amongst all 42 of us, but the obvious practicalities were impossible. My family had to come first.

I was one of only a few who would venture to the village. The others had been put off by Schmidt's words. That first encounter in the east Budapest railway station with a German officer had led me to believe I would always get away with my guise as a non-Jew. For the last year it had been, for the most part, foolproof.

On 6 May on my route into the village, I came across retreating German troops. Most had torn boots or no boots at all. The army of the Third Reich was now reduced to the existence their leaders had brought us. And I had an advantage over them, for my shoes, despite the huge distance they had travelled, were still intact.

A horse-drawn cart passed beside me. It was full of troops. One of the soldiers lifted up a bottle and held it out in my direction.

'Hey boy, do you want some wine?' he asked and laughed. The cart began to gather speed and I ran after it.

'Catch!' the soldier said, and he threw the bottle at me while the two horses pulling the cart increased their speed. I caught it and the cart pulled away from me. I opened the bottle but it contained cooking oil and not wine. However, that was no problem and most probably more useful. I could give it to my mother, collect wood for a fire and we could roast potatoes properly outside in the yard near our barn.

On the same day, I wandered to the end of the village where bricks and mortar gave way to open fields. I could see a single German army truck parked a stone's throw from the final house and some soldiers talking. I was ready to turn back when a soldier called to me: 'Hey boy, come here.'

I approached and he asked me if I wanted a cup of coffee. I replied: 'Yes, thank you,' and the soldier, a sergeant, handed me an aluminium cup filled with coffee from a silver-coloured jug. It was so hot I could not drink it in gulps and had to sip it slowly. As I drank, I noticed something strangely familiar under the canvas of the truck. I slowly realized that I was looking at Hebrew writing. It was a piece of the Torah, the five books of the Bible, and it was being used as a patch where the canvas was ripped. A sacred part of our Jewish heritage was being desecrated; it shocked me. I decided I must do something about it and finished my coffee quickly, thanked the sergeant and returned to the farm and the barn to find my father.

He was nowhere to be seen, and I felt I must tell someone of my discovery. Instead I told Uncle Joe who was a very religious man.

'Come with me and show me where it is,' he said.

I took him through the village and to the field where the friendly sergeant and the soldiers had been. As Uncle Joe and I approached the end of the street along which I had passed, we could both see that the troops were still parked in the field.

The sergeant was unperturbed by my return with another person. He cheekily asked: 'Hey boy, was the coffee so good that you brought your friend?'

The other soldiers laughed. My uncle asked him if he had a commanding officer and could he see him. A grey-haired captain came to meet us.

'What do you want?' the officer asked.

'Captain,' my uncle began in impeccable German, 'perhaps you don't know who we are? That piece of garment is part of our Bible,' and he pointed to the Torah, meshed into the canvas of the truck.

'If you could give it to us please?'

There was a pause and the captain looked at both of us contemptuously. I thought he was going to dismiss us, but he seemed to change his mind. He looked in the direction of the soldiers and beckoned one over.

'You see that thing there under the canvas, take it off! I don't want it here, but don't tear it. Roll it up and give it to this man.'

The soldier did as he was asked and the others looked on curiously as they witnessed him take from their truck what appeared to be some old rubbish fit only to plug a leak. For us it was holy and blasphemy to have it used as a huge patch.

It was rolled up and handed to my uncle.

'Thank you. Thank you very much Captain,' my uncle said earnestly.

We left and hurried back to our barn. As the two of us walked, I asked my uncle: 'Why weren't you afraid to ask a German officer a favour for a Jew?'

He replied, 'You know son, in 1939, in 1940 or in 1941, in the victorious years, I wouldn't have dared ask. But when I sneaked out from the farm yesterday I heard a villager's radio through the window of their house. The Russians were in the middle of Berlin. I knew that it was the end of Nazi Germany, so I had the guts to ask. The reality of the situation is that the Germans are defeated.'

'But Schmidt told us to stay away from retreating German troops, and to keep a low profile,' I reminded him. He was unperturbed.

'Those troops were few and friendly, not a badly disciplined mob,' he said.

My uncle carried the scroll lovingly. He sent me on ahead to get my father as he stood waiting near the farm. Uncle Joe did not want to cause a fuss by bringing the remnants of a Torah into the barn or yard where most of the others were gathered. He wanted to bury it quietly and that is what we did, with the help of my father, in a field outside the village.

Having done this, Uncle Joe and my father could now rest easy, knowing that, although it was not in its rightful place in a synagogue, the Torah scroll could no longer be desecrated.

12 In Search of Plenty

The area of Austria in which we were encamped had yet to be claimed by anyone. It was a no-man's-land with no recognized authority. On 8 May, the official end of the war in Europe, no army had yet occupied the little corner of Austria in which the 42 of us waited. Our collective hope was that one of the victors would reach us before any upset or disgruntled loser.

On 9 May I was woken by the familiar sound of army trucks. Who could it be? At first the fear of retreating and ill-disciplined German troops ran through my mind. More optimistically, it could be the Americans or Russians. That sudden thought excited me.

We could hear the purring of truck engines for a few minutes and then the sound of heavy boots jumping onto the ground. There was some talking in a language that was not familiar to me. By now, many more people had been woken in the barn.

Suddenly, the barn doors opened and the bright light of day broke into the darkened claustrophobic atmosphere of 42 people sleeping close together. Four silhouetted soldiers stood in the light, which had caused most of those not awake to rub their eyes and open them to see what was happening.

The soldiers were Russian and questioned the person nearest to the door, but he did not understand what they were saying. My dad stood up, dazed from just waking. He asked if anyone spoke Russian, but nobody answered. He then tried to speak with the soldiers. Having served in the Austro-Hungarian army during World War I he had come across many Slavic people and had fought in Serbia. Somehow he explained who we were. The Russian officer presumably accepted the explanation, although how he had understood, I do not know. I certainly did not understand and did not know if Russian had any similarity to Serbo-Croat.

However, whatever had been said and understood, the

troops were not taking any chances of letting the odd German soldier escape their justice. The officer looked on as the three private soldiers took a pitchfork each and began poking the hay. Apparently the officer thought there might be a German soldier or two hiding in there, keeping their secret at gunpoint. It all seemed a bit obsessive to me, but the Russians might well have had such previous experiences. Having found no one, the soldiers left the barn, got into their trucks and drove away.

Those who went into the village on subsequent days heard numerous rumours and locals complaining. Red Army troops had been picking up young women and dragging them away, especially during the night. Large numbers of young women were now hiding themselves away wherever they could or wearing kerchiefs to disguise their youthful looks. Women in the village looked drabber and less attractive, even the older women. Their hair seemed messier, their clothes untidy and they tried to avoid appearing in public. The Red Army troops had had an instant impact for the wrong reasons.

One night, Rusian soldiers came looking for a *zsenka* [a woman], amongst our tatty-looking and innocent group. My older sister Valerie was the youngest and prettiest of the women, who made up more than half of the 42 sleeping bodies in that barn, and so was a prime target. Those soldiers had only one thing on their mind: sex (i.e. rape).

The doors of the barn slowly and quietly opened and their torches were lights of terror, searching for a victim. They did not care if the woman had been victimized already by a previous ordeal or if she was a refugee – it was not a thought that crossed their minds. They were not thinking, only acting instinctively like animals. It was not even about some kind of tentative revenge against an Austrian or daughter of a Nazi leader. They wanted to feed their urge and now they came amongst us.

Everyone slept towards the middle and back of the barn away from the doors. It gave us that little bit of extra time. I do not think many people were asleep when the soldiers rudely interrupted the silence. Our traditional evening chat had petered out only 15 minutes or so earlier.

It was my younger sister Eva whose head rose from the hay first, quickly followed by my father and mother. Without a word, as if telepathic, all of my family had only one thought, and simultaneously, my older sister Valerie was frantically covered with hay by my mother, father, Eva and myself. I pressed her frame into the hay we were lying upon. Her feet still protruded and we whispered to her to curl her body slightly. Eva then lay on top of Valerie. I sat to my younger sister's left-hand side and my father swapped places with my mother and lay to her right.

We waited. The soldiers had delayed their search by some kind of discussion as they stood in the open doorway. Those were precious seconds. They now fanned out, to the left and right side of the barn. If they were searching for young women they were going to have difficulty finding them. Apart from my elder sister, the rest of the women were in their late forties or fifties. Only Eva, aged ten, and my second cousin, aged five, were younger.

Three soldiers crept over towards us. Eva and my father pretended to be asleep. I lay down, pretending to have just woken, as did my mother. Uncle Joe offered no such pretence and sat up. The soldiers passed by my mother, my father and Eva. They walked slowly past me, my uncles and their families. They crept by Joe who sat up and looked disdainfully into their eyes. They halted. Joe's sister sat blankly with her baby held to her chest. Everyone's eyes were fixed upon the three soldiers who had been joined by the rest, possibly another nine if my count had been correct. One soldier turned to another and said something no one could understand. There was a brief pause, and they turned and headed towards the open barn doors. Then they were gone.

One of our men stood up and joined by three others, made his way towards the doors. After looking out, they closed them. My father told my sister she could come out from the hay but to be ready to return if need be. She seemed unperturbed. My mother was nervous. I was shocked. Weren't those soldiers meant to be on our side? No one could sleep. The mood was fearful and angry. We stayed awake, just in case they tricked us and came back looking for someone they thought we had hidden. If those previous Red Army troops had poked the hay for errant Germans, then perhaps some others would do the same for women. As yet, though, the idea, or the desperation, was not there.

The following day about 50 or more Jews were brought under Red Army escort to the farm where we were staying. They too had the same complaint. Russian troops had come searching for young women. This topic seemed to hang in the air for days. Everyone who came in contact with us spoke about Russian soldiers looking for any young woman to rape. The farm now housed a hundred or so refugees. All of us had had to survive brutality at the hands of the German armed forces and their agents. Yet their conquerors and our supposed saviours were inflicting on us a new wave of fear and terror. I had a great interest in history. I knew civilians were always innocent victims. At the time, I thought that those men, women and children, who were now housed in one barn, had taken some of the worst punishment seen in the history of warfare. I did not know that at that point there were millions of people who had endured far worse conditions than we had. Why did those who had helped to bring our freedom have to mete out more trouble?

A day later, some men from our group marched off to the local commander, a Russian colonel, to complain. Our growing anger compelled us to take a stand. Everyone hoped that the Red Army had come to wash away the stain of the German menace, not to take its place as a brutal bully. But the colonel told our men he could not control his troops 24 hours a day. He said we should all leave for Znojmo, which was under Czech administration. The local Czech resistance were in charge, and there we would not have to fear the Russians. The local commander kindly offered disciplined troops as guards, who would escort us all from the village and on to Znojmo. We accepted his offer, thanked him and prepared that evening once more to walk into unknown territory.

By now the scope for obtaining handouts of food, either by *schnorrering* in the village or through the goodwill of the farmer had severely decreased. The Russian troops were using all available food supplies, as were an ever-increasing number of refugees, both non-Jewish and Jewish. So, as we made our way under escort to Znojmo, Czechoslovakia, once again we faced the problem of trying to make a journey on foot without enough to eat.

When we arrived at Znojmo, the Russian troops took us to a

school which served as a Czech administration centre. The Red Army was also present on this side of the border, but it was the former Czech resistance that ran the show. On the Austrian side of the border, the Soviet military was in charge, as Austria was now a slice of conquered 'Germany.'

The six soldiers who accompanied us spoke no German or Hungarian, and drove slowly along in their vehicles as our group of a hundred or so walked even slower. They were highly excitable and every few minutes they shouted, '*Hitler kaput! Germany kaput!*' [Hitler is finished! Germany is finished!] throughout our journey to Znojmo.

The Russian soldiers bade us farewell at the school, telling a poor Czech administrator that he now had about a hundred Jews on his hands. A mood of bitterness and disappointment towards our previous hosts was replaced by one of relief amongst our large group, now that we were under the supervision of the Czechs. I could not speak for everyone, but I felt a little more reassured about the Red Army. Our escorting soldiers had been very pleasant, but I did wonder about what they got up to at night.

We had no trouble communicating with our new Czech hosts. Some of those Jews who had joined us in the Austrian village just across the border were from areas of Czechoslovakia populated largely by ethnic Hungarians. However, the vast majority were from Vojvodina, an area of Yugoslavia with a sizeable Hungarian minority. All had been deported with most of the rest of Hungarian Jewry after the German invasion in March 1944. They had all been working in labour camps in Austria, mostly around Vienna. A handful though were from southern Hungary and amongst these we had found a cousin, Helen, and her 18-year-old daughter Agnes. All the 11 members of my family who were present knew them well and were on good terms with them. Meeting again in that small Austrian village was entirely unexpected, but a very pleasant surprise. Helen's husband had been another casualty of the Munkatabor, killed on the Eastern Front.

The Czech administrators quickly organized for all hundred or so of us to stay in former Nazi villas. Four villas were up for grabs and we were told to make our own groups of family and friends. We were all excited at the prospect of actually staying in a proper house, even though we could not guess what sort of state it would be in. Our family group now numbered 13. Along with some friends of Helen and Agnes, we gathered together a group of 22. I was separated from Joe, Mr Biederman, Mr Ziegelman, Mr Adler and Uncle Kiss for the first time in almost a year. However, separation only meant not sleeping in the same room, as their villa was next to ours. In fact all four villas were next to each other. These splendid buildings were situated along a street that led directly to the station. The street was lined with trees and gave an impression of vast suburban wealth. However, it was pock-marked with bomb craters, which spoiled the splendour. Despite their state of abandonment, the villas were still magnificent to look at: I had never before seen such buildings.

The villa we were to occupy had three floors and a cellar. The previous resident had been a Nazi functionary. Wasn't it ironic, I thought, that those they had wanted to kill now slept in their vacated houses. The garden of our villa had a large bomb crater and the windows opening onto it were smashed. However, the local authorities fixed them with plywood within 24 hours of our arrival. The rest of the building's windows were intact.

We were pleasantly surprised, for the inside of the villa was very clean with most of the furnishings in place. It was convenient that the Nazi bosses had lived so close to the station. They had fled when the Russians had approached, taking what they could with them. Only portable items had been taken, although someone had obviously thought about taking blankets and sheets as they were piled on the beds, the sheets beautifully white and ironed.

The villa was equipped with everything you might expect. The kitchen had every utensil, pot, pan and plate. The cupboards contained flour, sugar, salt and spices. The house had electric lights that worked, clothes and even a flushing toilet. It was a paradise, an Aladdin's cave; it was everything you could wish for after a year without a proper bed, proper food or somewhere to wash. There was a bath with running water, although there was not any hot water. There were carpets, sofas and a soft pillow to lay your head on. What luxury! What pleasure! What bliss! It is impossible to put it into words.

As we walked around and discovered this big house, I thought of a biblical passage that stated, 'What you sow you shall reap.' Those influential Nazis who had left in such a hurry had been the agents of our destruction. We had been forced out at short notice from our homes with only those items we could carry. The Nazis who had lived in this villa and others like it across formerly occupied Europe had had to do the same. History had come full circle.

Agnes and I went in search of anything we could find to eat. On the top floor Agnes suddenly shouted, 'Come quick!'

In one of the cupboards she had found cherries preserved in rum. There were 30 big jars of cherries. It was a great find. As there was also plenty of flour and sugar, my mother and some other women began to make cakes.

That first evening in the villa, we chatted and feasted on cakes. Some of us even had a bed to sleep on, but 22 people could not share them all! Some slept on a sofa, but as a young male I drew the short straw and slept upon the carpeted floor. It did not matter. I felt contented and relaxed. We had better food, proper shelter and conveniences I was not even used to at home, like a flushing toilet. It was almost heavenly. And it would have been so if I had had a bed!

Despite the fact that food had been left by the previous owners of the villas, the Czech authorities served meals twice a day for refugees at the school we had been taken to on our arrival in Znojmo. The town did not house many refugees though. It was modern-looking, and besides damage near the train station, the war had not inflicted too much destruction upon it.

We travelled into town in groups, happily as free people. However, there was nothing to attract young or old. The war had recently finished, so what could there be? The shops were empty, people milled around and the Czechs were still capturing those Germans who had not fled in time. On one occasion a group of us witnessed two young people, a boy and a girl, scream at three young German women they had found. The boy held his rifle and the girl, with the Germans' hands raised above their heads, beat their legs with a stick. She screamed and screamed and screamed. Revenge was in the air. I assumed this scene was being repeated across Europe.

The local Czechs had obviously had a bad time at the hands of their German conquerors. Perhaps that was an understatement. (My family and I certainly had not had a good time!) Two incidents, one involving my older sister and the other involving myself, illustrate this.

One day Valerie was wandering around the town with her friends. She was wearing Tyrolean socks – popular clothing which originated in southern Germany, associated with places such as Bavaria and the Tyrol. She stopped by the local militia who ordered her to 'take off those German-looking things!' She replied that she was Jewish, so why should she be picked upon. They told her, 'All the more reason to take them off!' She was then made to take off the socks, while her friends looked on. The socks were taken away by the militia. Valerie came home later, a slightly bewildered person.

The second occasion was potentially rather more serious. I was strolling in town with Joe, when I was stopped for wearing a Tyrolean hat.

'What's that on your head?' one youth armed with a sub-machine gun shouted to me.

I was tempted to reply, 'a hat', but the boy had a companion who was also armed. I had not known what to reply, but fortunately he asked,

'Why are you wearing that German hat?'

'I like wearing it,' I said.

It was not a good reply. I had prided myself on being able to avoid detection by German soldiers because I had brown hair and blues eyes, those 'assets' in this circumstance now had the opposite effect. I had also responded in German. Consequently, I was told at gunpoint that I was under arrest and the hat snatched from my head. I was a suspected German youth. Joe was left unmolested and he returned to my parents to tell them the news.

I was taken to the military headquarters where I was brought before a Czech army colonel. He told me that my appearance, and the fact I had begun to speak to the militia in German, aroused suspicion. I told him that I was a Jewish refugee staying in a villa near the station and that German was the only way to communicate with the armed youths. He gave me back the hat and asked me not to wear it again. To complete the black comedy, I told him I did not know the way back to the villa in which I was staying, so he sent one of the militia men who had arrested me to show me the way back. I arrived safely and told my parents my latest adventure.

'A little nationalistic outburst,' my father said.

'It's understandable a few weeks after the end of the war.'

I could not speak for all of Czechoslovakia, but certain incidents such as these seemed to show that the Czechs hated anything that reminded them of the Germans. It appeared a little oversensitive to me, despite the way I myself had been treated, but understandable.

Despite these incidents, our stay at Znojmo was a step up from our former existence. The weather became warmer and warmer, the days sunnier and life altogether rosier. The children played in the gardens of the villas. There was laughter – something that had been missing for a long while. Perhaps the days seemed much warmer and sunnier than they really were, but if that was so it was due to our new-found freedom.

After two weeks at the villa in Znojmo, all hundred or so of us were ordered to leave for Brno. The villa had been comfortable, but we now had to move. Before we left, the Czech authorities called us all into an abandoned German army warehouse, where a huge amount of clothing and bedwear had been left by the fleeing German armed forces. We were allowed to take warm socks, blankets and anything else we might need for the coming journey. (These items could replace some of those clothes we had lost through wear and tear.) I chose a very warm German army coat and a German army sweater. We could not take too much or carry too much. There were plenty of others who needed the same items from the same warehouse, but we took what we could. It was spring, the end of May, but the nights were still cold.

As we made the short journey to the station from the villas, there was yet more irony in the way many of our group were dressed. I wore a German army coat, another wore German army boots, another German army trousers. What would those armed youths who had arrested me have made of this?

As we all boarded the train, we had seats to sit on, not cattle trucks to stand in. All of us had been well fed, well looked after and clothed. Our Znojmo hosts had taken good care of us, and on a sunny day we departed on a journey which would take us deep into Czechoslovakia.

Despite Brno being only about 60 kilometres from Znojmo, the train journey took several hours. The aftermath of war kept the speed of train travel at a snail's pace. The journey seemed to take longer because of our unwelcome company. All hundred or so of us had boarded a regular train with some extra carriages. My parents, sisters and I were quietly sitting in one compartment until our peace was disturbed by a Russian major and his adjutant. The major was drunk.

The Russian soldiers had boarded the train at Znojmo. At first the major began chatting with a young woman in the next compartment. She had obviously rejected his advances and they began arguing. The adjutant tried to calm him down and she left for another carriage. He then entered our compartment, followed by his dutiful adjutant. The major, swaying somewhat, placed his hand on my father's shoulder and said, 'Germany kaput. Harasho?'

He was tall, broad and looked too young to be a major. In one hand he held a bottle of vodka and in the other a pistol. He sat down opposite my father and placed his gun on the table that divided us.

All my family were very quiet. The major held out the bottle of vodka and said some words which probably meant, 'Do you want a drink?' My father took the bottle and poured some vodka in his army cup which he had collected from the warehouse in Znojmo. (We all had taken one.) He took a sip of the vodka. The major then offered me a drink. I gestured to him, 'no', but my mother turned to me and said, 'Drink a little, don't offend him. He may get angry. We don't know if the gun is loaded.'

So, I poured some vodka into my cup and sipped it. My first taste of alcohol and my mother was encouraging me to drink! He then offered the bottle to my mother, but my father told him, '*Zsenka, nyet*' [woman, no], and he got the message.

The major then began rolling off stories, although my father could only recognize the words, 'wife' and 'children', amongst his fuddled ramblings. Throughout all this, his adjutant, another tall and broad man, sat nervously – too embarrassed to speak.

Eventually two men from the Czech militia joined us all for a 'chat'. We were relieved and knew they had come to remedy the situation. At the second stop of our journey to Brno, one militia man left our compartment, climbed onto the platform and called the Russian military police. Two of them visited our compartment, coolly asked the major to join them and took his pistol. The drunken officer and his adjutant left, giving us some peace. The major had never been threatening, but we had felt decidedly uncomfortable in his presence, especially as he had been armed. Yet again, another representative of the army that had freed eastern Europe had left much to be desired. However, I hoped that despite such first impressions these incidents involved merely a minority of men among a majority of the great and good.

13 The Return Home

At last we arrived in Brno, the second largest city in Czechoslovakia. The city thronged with people. It appeared to be a stopping point for refugees of various nationalities. There was a tired but euphoric atmosphere as liberated foreigners moved amongst celebrating locals.

In the evening it was warm, but the atmosphere on the streets was even warmer. In the squares, the locals danced in the open air, flaunting their new freedom with their saviours, the soldiers of the Red Army. Here the mood was of delirious happiness, and the troops of the Soviet armed forces were welcome companions and not the fearful bullies we had encountered across the border in Austria.

This time we had no private villas: there were too many displaced people in the city. Instead, we were housed in a school with hundreds more refugees.

It was time to say goodbye to Joe and his family, Mr Biederman, Mr Ziegelman, Mr Adler and Uncle Kiss. They had to return to their own towns and discover what had become of their relatives. We hugged and kissed, hoping to see each other again.

All 13 members of our family were still together, but familiar faces were leaving us. We walked around Brno but did not want to stray too far from the school in case we got lost. We were no longer part of a large group of Jews, who were placed in a small or medium-sized town and could rely upon one another if things went wrong. Now each of us was just another face in the crowd. We felt lost in the huge numbers of people that surrounded us.

From being merely a yellow star we became merely 'next'. Next in the line for a meal ticket which gave us food for two meals a day. Next in the line for a medical check-up and given DDT. There was endless queuing, while new arrivals were

naturally served first. We were thankful that someone somewhere cared enough to give us food or check our health, but it
was all a little disappointing. It was like being on a conveyor belt:
another statistic, not a person. But what else could the authorities
do?

Brno had been damaged little by the war. It was an old city
and its architecture projected an aura of greater things than a
huge refugee camp. The aftermath of war had resulted in large
numbers of raggedly dressed people. One man who stood out in
my memory sat in the street not far from the school. He
appeared mad, to say the least, with wild dirty white hair, an
unshaven face and gaps in his teeth. The man sat barefooted,
rags around his very skinny body, laughing bizarrely. People
would walk past and barely notice him, perhaps only giving him
a glance. Then one day he was gone. Some police had taken him
away. When I asked a policeman where the mad old man had
gone, he told me that the man had in fact 'been in hiding'. They
had discovered a 'G' tatooed in his armpit – a sign that he was a
member of the Gestapo. Whatever had happened to him had
driven the man mad. I had originally felt sad for that bizarre person who sat on the street, alone, but on discovering he was from
the Gestapo, I no longer felt pity. I knew the Gestapo had caused
unspeakable suffering. Rumours of murder and horror were rife
throughout the refugee centre.

At the centre, we met many who had been interned in
Auschwitz, Buchenwald, Dachau or Bergen Belsen. They were
returning to their homes in the bordering countries, including
Hungary. Discussions centred around, 'How was your place?' or
'I'm from such and such a town, did you meet so and so from
such and such a place?' People were looking for any clue as to
the whereabouts of their relatives and friends. At first we could
not believe the stories these people were telling us. The BBC and
the *Washington Post* had refused to believe even their own eyes
at the first uncovered death camp, Majdanek, in eastern Poland,
where the Russians had brought in foreign correspondents to
witness the horror. Yet, as the accounts and the shocked state of
many became overwhelming, we realized how incredibly lucky
we had been. We were much skinnier, but people we met had
lost whole families and had been unimaginably dehumanized. I
had just spent the worst months of my life, and yet I had been

very fortunate. All of us wondered if any of our relatives and friends had been interned or killed.

It was difficult to get a seat on a train, and we waited for more than a week before we boarded one going towards Bratislava. People desperate to get home were willing to hop onto anything pulled by a locomotive. With our baggage, the 13 members of our family boarded cattle-trucks. They had taken us out of Hungary and they were now returning us. Not enough train carriages in postwar Europe meant the same trucks that had taken Jews to their slaughter took the survivors home again. People sat on the roofs of train carriages if no further space inside was available. Alternatively, we sat, like many more, in open cattle-trucks.

Our train journey took us through beautiful countryside and when we arrived in Bratislava there was another pleasant surprise: we did not have to stay. There were spaces on the train for Budapest, so hours after our arrival, our next train rolled towards Hungary. We all wondered how our country would now look.

As we passed through western Hungary, the towns showed the price of war. The evidence of destruction was everywhere. The western side of the Danube had seen bitter fighting, some towns changing sides three or four times between the German and Soviet armies. The famous bridges that connected the Buda half of Budapest to the Pest half were destroyed and their twisted remains lay in the Danube. Traffic crossed by means of pontoon bridges made by the Red Army. Most of Buda, the western half of Budapest, lay in ruins – the result of three-months' fighting.

On our arrival, members of the Jewish Agency met us as we got off the train. We were led through a ruined city marked by rubble and buildings pock-marked with bullet holes. The city had seen house-to-house, flat-to-flat and floor-to-floor fighting. Some called it the second Stalingrad. Some had also called Budapest 'Judapest', because its population had been one-quarter Jewish. I doubted that the city was one-quarter Jewish anymore.

Located in Klauzal Square was the Jewish Agency. Notable as a 'Jewish district' before the war, it now housed some of the remnants of a once-thriving community, returning sullen and saddened.

Along with the other Jewish refugees we were again sprayed with DDT and given a medical examination. Clothes and shoes were offered if we wanted them. I threw some of my worn trousers, shirts and a pair of shoes away and took some of those on offer. Everyone also received a train ticket for their home-town. Once again, countless strangers approached us, asking if we had seen their relatives. My family had arrived in Klauzal Square more than a month after the war's end, yet so many were clutching at straws while looking in a haystack. These refugees were still searching in desperate hope of finding their mother or father, sister or brother, son or daughter, grandchil-dren, cousin, husband or wife. Many would continue to do so for months and years ahead.

Uncle Eugene went in search of his second daughter, Elizabeth, who had been living in Budapest before the Germans had invaded. There was only one place to begin: at her address of March 1944. He expected little and to be told she had been taken elsewhere. To his astonishment, the door of the flat was opened by his granddaughter. She and Elizabeth had both been in hiding in Budapest and had returned to their home once the Red Army had captured the city. It was a very joyful reunion, and along with his wife and other daughter Anna and grand-daughter, they moved in temporarily to Elizabeth's flat. It was a cramped but happy home.

Uncle Joe and Aunt Rene left for their home-town, as did Agnes and her mother, so we had a tearful goodbye. Everyone hoped to see each other again soon in better circumstances and with missing friends and relatives safely returned.

We stayed in Budapest for only a few days to register our arrival back in Hungary. Thousands of people were coming and going; they were wandering in huge numbers, the multitude was impossible to imagine had one not been present. Everyone was rushing back to familiar surroundings and familiar faces after years of upheaval.

Our minds turned to how our home town would look. Had it been damaged? Had it changed? Had the people changed? My family had not changed visibly or indeed psychologically, as far as I could judge. But maybe on their inside, it was different. I know it was for me. I felt more grown up, more confident of doing things on my own. I was now sixteen, but felt more like a man with the kind of experience I would not have wished for, nor would wish on anyone else. At least I had not experienced the awful horrors that others had. However, I felt bitter at having had so little food for so long, at having to survive by begging, and indeed at all I had experienced. These months had changed me forever in one more inevitable way. From now on, waste of any kind, especially food, was worse than a red rag to a bull for me; it was abhorrent. This was understandable. But what was going on in the minds of those who had survived death camps, I dared not think. In a world that has so many hungry mouths to feed, I have always appreciated every meal and instilled in my children to do the same. Yet, I was fortunate that so many people in Mistelbach had been willing to give help. I was fortunate to have been in Mistelbach.

The regular three-hour journey took eight hours. The train needed several stops for water and repairs. It seemed to echo the feelings of so many people on the train: worn out, in need of proper rest and recuperation and somewhere familiar for life-giving rejuvenation.

As the train approached Kiskunhalas, we could see that the town had escaped the great damage and destruction of western Hungary and Budapest. The lightning Red Army offensive of October 1944 had overrun Kiskunhalas, advancing from Romania in the southeast. The town had surrendered too quickly for any large-scale damage, and only a handful of buildings and bomb craters betrayed the signs of war.

At Kiskunhalas's small railway station there was a big welcome. Jewish community representatives were waiting for us. After some greetings and 'glad to see you' conversations, it was down to business. Part of the synagogue had been turned into a warehouse. Any furniture or utensils we needed would be delivered the same day. The illegal occupiers of our home had been thrown out.

At last, my family and I had arrived at the street that had been our home for so long but from which we had been wrenched more than a year before. Our number was one less. The moment was bitter-sweet.

Our spectacle of leaving was more dramatic than our return. Julia saw us entering our house once more and was very happy to see us. Bringing her two daughters with her, she ran over and greeted us, giving my mother a big hug. Julia sent one of her daughters back to collect bread and fruit for us all. She had kept those belongings we had given her for the day of our return and kept her word, handing each one back. The bed linen and dishes which we had given her now came in handy. Julia's family illustrated the good side of human nature. She asked about grandmother, but we could only tell her the worst and then about our experiences. Others had suffered worse things than us. We had been lucky, but she already knew of the terrible facts.

For my parents, sisters and myself, it was good, naturally, to be back home after having endured so many journeys and uncomfortable places during the past months. However, our experiences, the death of our grandmother, worry over missing relatives and the state in which we found our house meant our return was more businesslike than euphoric or nostalgic. Our house had been defiled.

In April 1944 we had left a comfortable home. In July 1945 we returned to four bare walls. Everything was gone. All that was left were some scraps of wood where a wall cabinet once stood, while the huge numbers of books that once filled it were now just a handful scattered upon the floor. The only other item to remain was the kitchen stove. Our home had been stripped bare. I began to search for my big stamp album that I had forgotten to give to a non-Jewish friend because of our hurried departure. I had been stamp-collecting for years and there were more than 2,000 stamps in the album.

'My stamp album – it's gone,' I told my father.

'Listen, there are more important things lost in this war,' he replied.

However, the stamp album had been something I had painstakingly built up, from as early as I could remember. It was my treasure. I had stupidly believed, before entering them, that it would still be within those four walls. It was the icing on the cake, but the cake had a bitter taste and the icing too. I could only sigh and agree with my father. I resigned myself to the fact that the stamp album had gone. More important things had been lost. The war was over, and that was what counted most.

A member of a local Jewish committee visited soon after and asked us what we needed. Some furniture, including a wardrobe and beds, were delivered. We asked for pots, pans and kitchen utensils so we could cook some food. The synagogue was situated a few minutes from our house, so delivery was not difficult.

The warehouse contained a compendium of items which the fleeing Nazis had in their possession: belongings they had stolen from others, most probably Jews. Some of the furniture the committee gave us had originally been ours anyway. They simply handed back some of our stolen possessions.

The following day the neighbour that supplied us with honey brought wine to celebrate our safe return. We began to fraternize with our former neighbours once more, as we had done before our deportation. They told us that they were glad to see us again and had read in the newspaper what had happened to Jews. That was all they were willing to say in conversation. Then they would tell us, 'I must be going.' It was as if they were too horrified or ashamed to hear anymore.

Twice a week a train arrived at Kiskunhalas. All of my family, including myself, went to the station to see if any new faces returned from the camps in Germany and former occupied Europe. We met every train that arrived at Kiskunhalas station until the end of September, waiting to see who would return. Little by little a few did, but only a few, worn out and melancholy. As they returned, the numbers of people making the pilgrimage to the station increased, as more survivors waited and hoped.

A 16-year-old Jewish school friend of mine arrived back in Kiskunhalas in late August. I asked him where his parents and sister were, but he did not know. He had been separated from them the day we had left Kiskunhalas and taken to a factory. When the war was drawing to a close, he was marched, along with hundreds of other Jews, for days in one last attempt to kill their number, even in the throes of the Nazi defeat. When the march was halted by an Allied air attack on the convoy, he had taken his chance in the commotion and escaped. A guard had shot him in the leg during the escape and he walked for many kilometres, injured and losing blood, surviving only on berries. For five days he stumbled on before meeting the advancing Red

Army forces. They fed him and attended to his bullet wound. Then they put him on a train for Hungary. Nevertheless, he had been held up and quarantined in transit camps, eventually arriving home after my family and I. He waited a year for his family, hoping that they would return. Sadly they never did, and he had to come to terms with the fact that they were most probably dead.

As peace settled we tried to find out which members of our large extended family had returned to their home towns and which had not. It would take longer to discover who was dead than who was living. Those who were missing with no trace of where they had gone could still be alive, or they could well be dead. Missing equalled uncertainty, but there was hope. We still waited for either the good news or the worst possible news. Too many of my uncles, aunts, cousins and friends were missing. We could only wait and see.

A second cousin working in the Munkatabor found himself in a village in western Hungary while marching towards Germany. He too escaped in the commotion of an air attack and asked a local farmer to hide him in return for five hectares of his father's land, who was also a farmer. The farmer agreed and he was hidden for two months before the Red Army arrived. After the war, the promise was quickly honoured, only for the communists to confiscate the land of all farmers a few years later.

A non-blood relative had survived through (planned) bribery. My mother's third brother Leopold and his brother-in-law, also called Leopold, were together in the Munkatabor. One particular day their group was permitted to drink in a tavern for a rest. As usual they were told they could have a 20-minute break, but instead were suddenly called to return after about only ten minutes. My mother's brother insisted on returning to the group but his brother-in-law wanted to remain for the whole of the 20 minutes. He did so, and not missing him, the Munkatabor group left without him. However, brother-in-law Leopold now feared being shot as a deserter from the Munkatabor. He wandered about, until he noticed a Hungarian army truck, parked and pointed in the direction of Budapest. A young lieutenant sat in the truck. The wandering Leopold offered the young officer 350 gold Napoleonic coins (which were hidden under the floorboards of his house) if he would take him to Budapest where the Red Army was advancing. The lieutenant accepted. He drove and drove through one check-point after the next until coming to a major military checkpoint run by the military police just before Budapest. However, it was too risky to take Leopold through this one. Instead, the lieu-tenant advised him to wait until dark, escape into the nearby orchards and only to travel at night. He told Leopold that he did not want any gold coins. His family were poor and their Jewish dentist had always waived any cost of treatment. One good turn deserved another.

Leopold took the advice of the young lieutenant – he escaped into the orchards and walked all night until reaching his home town, Vacz. He was hidden by a friend and waited ten days before the Red Army liberated that area of western Hungary. However, on returning to the house, the wine merchant who had stored the gold coins as an anti-inflationary war measure, found them gone. At least he had his life though. The other Leopold, it was later discovered, was dead.

And so the stories of turmoil and survival quickly found audi-ences who could tell their own and relieve the burden of their experiences. Another second cousin survived by joining the Russian partisans after fleeing the Munkatabor, and he arrived back in Hungary in a Red Army uniform. Some more relatives survived hidden in Budapest, living a nerve-racking existence. These were the stories of history to be told and retold for decades and generations to come.

For weeks after our arrival back in Kiskunhalas the days passed lazily. The house was cleaned, mended and organized. We were picking up pieces, both literally and metaphorically. It was now peacetime and life would have to continue with some sem-blance of normality. Only the passage of time could restore this. The education committee decided that those children who had missed school because of the war would study anew, with the school year beginning in January and not September as usual. (I was not in the mood to study in September and nor would I be in January.) Those children taken away would be given lenient marking for examinations and school work. We could expect nothing less.

It was time to be a teenager again. The past 18 months had changed me mentally and emotionally. I had faced challenges daunting for any adult, but it was time to put being an adult on hold.

As we stood in the small Kiskunhalas synagogue on Rosh Hashana, the Jewish New Year, an air of sadness hung over the small congregation. Once vibrantly singing their prayers, they now seemed to be just going through the motions. Formerly, the small Kiskunhalas Jewish community had filled the synagogue to capacity on holy days. Now its numbers were vastly depleted. There was an eerie emptiness around us as we prayed. Familiar faces were absent; all of those present had lost family members and anxiously waited for news of the missing.

On the second evening of the two-day celebration of the Jewish New Year, everyone in the synagogue could hear gunshots from outside. The shots came from a civil servant's home, who lived in a hacienda-style house nearby. He owned three dogs: Stalin, Churchill and Roosevelt. This was no compliment. In Hungary at this time, to name a dog after a person was the worst kind of insult one could give. A supporter of the Axis powers, after their defeat, he renamed the dogs Hitler, Mussolini and Franco. He dare not call the dogs by their old names, especially with Russian troops occupying the town, although they failed to obey commands to their new ones. A drunken soldier had jumped over the civil servant's fence, trying to steal wine from his cellar. The three dogs had jumped on him but he had shot them. That drunken Russian soldier had done what no assassin could accomplish – he had killed Stalin, Churchill and Roosevelt in one fell swoop!

During the following days, I prayed in the morning with my father during the so-called 'Ten Days of Penitence', which lead up to the holiest day of the Jewish year. We were praying for ourselves and everyone else, living and dead. If the Nazis had wanted to prevent this very sight, Jews praying, still having faith and following their culture, then they had been defeated not only in battle but also in the mind. Our synagogue illustrated that. I hoped others across Europe also did.

The holiest day of the Jewish year arrived: Yom Kippur, the Day of Atonement – the first in peacetime for six years. The Day of

Atonement was more sombre than usual, for obvious reasons. Had those people missing from our synagogue and all the others up and down Europe sinned so badly that they deserved to be mocked, brutalized, experimented upon, shot, gassed or victimized in a host of other ways? Had their dead bodies deserved to be desecrated? As I stood in the Yom Kippur service I remembered the prayer that stated, 'G-d will love those that love Him and will punish their enemies.'

Then what had gone so terribly wrong? Also, as so many others have asked, 'Where was G-d?'

The scenes across Europe were apocalyptic. Starting with the Russian discovery of Majdenek death camp in eastern Poland and ending with their liberation of Theresienstadt in Czechoslovakia, the world discovered that the rumours were true. The advance of technology in the hands of the wicked could massacre millions of people. The Jews had been singled out and systematically exterminated. They were not alone. Political prisoners, homosexuals, the disabled, civilians from various nationalities, hundreds of thousands of Soviet Prisoners of War and Romany people had also been ruthlessly murdered.

Then we came to the most moving part of the service, the prayer for the dead, Kaddish. I could only hope, and I am sure the rest of our small Kiskunhalas congregation would have agreed, that some of its words would hold true:

'*Yihei Shlamah Rabah Min Shmaiya vchaim tovim aleinu.*' [May there be abundant peace from heaven and a happy life for us.]

Amen.

Epilogue

The train crawled into Mistelbach station. I had brought my mother and sister to face a haunting memory from the past. They had not complained when I had told them where I proposed our journey would be. 'All right', they said, somewhat indifferently. They had not tried to dissuade me.

Why had I come? Was it simply a morbid sense of curiosity? Did I merely want to see what had become of little Mistelbach-ander-Zaya? I had even brought a camera.

In fact it was not curiosity, idle or otherwise, that had led me to return. I wanted to walk as a free man in Mistelbach where once I had walked as a slave. I wanted to meet any pro-Nazi I had come into contact with, tell them what bastards they were, and walk away without fear of someone arresting me. I wanted to meet anyone of those people who had been so kind to me and given me food, when their discovery by a Nazi sympathizer could have landed them in very serious trouble. I wanted to return to Mistelbach for the practical purposes of dignity, revenge and thanks.

I knew my way through town well, but only from the main square, so we took a taxi there. The town had changed, but not dramatically. Many of the shops had changed owners or sold different goods. The new sixties' consumer had arrived, and some shops sold televisions or refrigerators. It was an altogether modern look that made it different from the place I remembered in 1945. However, the town seemed still to be about the same size, and as the taxi approached the square, the familiar tower of the church remained. The square had changed though. As one might have guessed, it was no longer called the 'Hitler Platz'. Instead, its former name before the Anschluss, the 'Hauptplatz', had been restored.

First, I decided, I wanted to see Richter – a Nazi supporter who

121

had chased me from his shop and had shouted the standard terms of abuse at me as a Jew. If I went to his shop I could tell him what I really thought of him, and he would not be able to call his Nazi chums to arrest me. He wouldn't be able to throw me out of his shop for the 'crime' of wanting to buy some food, although now I had no wish to purchase anything. When I had entered his shop all those years before, I had not known its owner was a Nazi supporter. If I had, I probably would not have gone there.

Richter's name no longer adorned the grocery shop. I went inside while my mother and sister remained outside. The bell over the door rang as it had done 17 years before. The owner came out from the room behind the counter. She was friendly and in her late twenties.

'What do you want to buy?' she asked.

'I don't want to buy anything,' I told her. 'Is Richter here?'

'Sorry. He died three years ago,' she replied.

The woman and her husband had taken over the shop.

'Mrs Richter comes in occasionally. If you're a friend or acquaintance, I'll give her a message,' she said.

'I'm not a friend and I'm not an acquaintance. I knew him during the war. I have no message.'

I walked out. I had been unsuccessful in meeting Richter and telling him he was a bastard, but at least I knew he was dead.

Next I took my mother and sister to the glass and mirror shop where I had bought a glass for a naptha lamp. The shop had been adorned with Himmler and Goring pictures. Again, I entered the shop alone. (Obviously, there were no Nazi pictures on this occasion.) A woman from behind the counter asked me what I wanted, but I told her I was just looking. I stayed a few minutes and left.

My third destination was a vegetable shop I had visited several times on my daring 'missions' to buy some groceries. It was still there, but had changed ownership. This being the case, I decided not to linger.

We made our way back to the Hauptplatz and from there found once more the path that led to the Forstgarten. There were no yellow stars, no hiding, no fear. I felt as if a part of me had been restored.

On the way we met a farmer. I asked him if he knew Philipi Netti. By chance he did, but he told us that the Italian restaurant-owner had died. I asked about Brussman and Mitzi. He knew them too. Brussman had died two years ago. As for Mitzi, she had got married, but that was all he knew.

Eventually we reached the road and then the bridge that led to those two wooden buildings that had been our 'home' during so many months of World War II. The Forstgarten looked exactly the same: the large wooden barn, the small wooden barn, the fences, the people working in the fields. Before we reached the gate, a woman in her thirties approached us.

'What do you want?' she asked.

I told her we had been prisoners during the war and where she now worked had been our camp. She was friendly and showed all three of us inside those wooden buildings. They were now warehouses for various items, including tools. It appeared that the Forstgarten was still a horticultural centre.

I took some photographs with my mother and sister, and then we walked back towards the Hauptplatz. On the way, we stopped at the house where the little girl lived, who all those years before would give me potatoes on the way back from work in town. I knocked on the door and a woman in her twenties answered. Could this be the little girl? I asked her if she knew of the farmer and her daughter. However, I was told that as far as the woman knew, the girl was now married and had moved away with her mother.

On reaching the Hauptplatz we stopped for a bite of food. There was no need to stay much longer; I had seen what I had wanted to see and I had dragged my mother and sister around for long enough.

At the Hauptplatz we flagged down a taxi to take us to the station. From inside it I saw the name 'Dunkler' posted outside a construction yard. Whoever it belonged to, the firm was still in the family.

We waited at Mistelbach train station for an hour before the train for Vienna arrived. I was a little disappointed. I had not met anyone I had wanted to meet. I could not let out my feelings: to curse or to show my gratitude. But at least I could put one ghost to rest. I had walked as an equal through town, and that had been as important as the other two put together.

123

Sheer luck had played a large part in the survival of those people, myself included, who had lived in the Forstgarten in Mistelbach. All of us had been thankful that we had survived and not been interned in one of those camps which we had learned of on our return to Hungary: the infamous names within whose walls unimaginable horrors had been perpetrated. We had discovered on our eventual arrival back in our home-towns, that so many of our loved ones had been murdered.

Uncle Kiss had returned home only to find that his wife had been killed in Auschwitz, the most notorious of Nazi death camps. His only son had died while on the Eastern Front with the Munkatabor. A lost and lonely man, he died of a broken heart just six months after the end of the war.

Mr Reinitz, who had escaped while we had marched through the Austrian countryside, also returned safely to Soltvadkert. He too only found sadness. His wife and four children had all died in Auschwitz, but continuing with his life he later remarried.

As for Mr Biederman, Mr Ziegelman and Mr Adler, I do not know what became of them, only that their wish to survive had been granted. Mr Biederman's wish for justice and Mr Ziegelman's desire for revenge were both fulfilled to a certain extent. Many pro-Nazi supporters were either imprisoned or executed. As for the German population of many Hungarian towns, they were forced to leave because of the ill-feeling towards anything Germanic. It was likely that Mr Ziegelman may well have watched those who had sneered at him and told him he would not return leave against their will. Yet again, history had turned full circle.

Joe returned to his home-town and restarted his father's haulage business. His married sister, brother-in-law and nephew moved to Austria to begin their life anew.

My mother's family, at first appeared to have led a charmed life. Her children and husband, along with two of her brothers and their families, had found themselves in a difficult but not life-threatening camp to those sound in body and mind, located in the Austrian lowlands. That day we had stood amongst thousands of Jews in Szeged and decided which cattle-truck to board had been a day of fortune, not bad luck. The first 30 cattle-trucks were taken to Auschwitz. My uncles, my father and I had boarded the first truck of the second 30 at the last moment. Later we discovered that it too had been travelling to Auschwitz. But it had turned back. At the time we had not known where we were heading, or why the trucks had changed direction. During the postwar years, the name of one man, Raul Wallenberg, featured in the possible solutions as to why we had escaped the most notorious of Nazi death camps.

One story told of how he had bribed senior German officials who had sent the second set of 30 cattle-trucks to labour camps instead of Auschwitz. The second was of Raul Wallenberg actually disguising himself as a high-ranking German official and changing the route of the train.

In searching for an answer to our miracle, the legend of Raul Wallenberg appeared to be the only possible explanation. My family and many others wanted to thank someone, but perhaps the lesser-known figures of Rudolph Kastner and Joel Brand might have been more appropriate. Kastner, a Hungarian Jew, and his partner, Joel Brand, organized a deal with top Nazi officials to barter 18,000 Jews for, amongst other things, coffee and soup. The cattle-trucks in which these Jews had been transported were diverted from their original destination, Auschwitz, to Austria. An estimated 16,000 survived the war. Whether Raul Wallenberg was responsible for our miracle, or Kastner and Brand, or indeed whether it was due to something else entirely, we still do not know. Whatever the truth, I am sure it would not be presumptuous to say that all the survivors were truly grateful. The whole incident was unusual to say the least.

Uncle Joe returned safely to begin his life once more as a head teacher, and his wife Rene became head of education for her district, encompassing 22 schools. Uncle Eugene started his watch-making business again. However, my mother's family had not in fact escaped misery. Her four sisters, together with their husbands and children, were all killed in Auschwitz. Her other brother, Leopold, had died in Mathausen concentration camp near Linz.

My father's family also suffered a terrible toll. Three sisters and one brother were all killed in Auschwitz. Only one brother remained. He had managed to hide in Budapest under a false name, and along with his wife, daughter and son, survived to rebuild their printing business.

Postwar Europe was all about starting over again, new

buildings, new jobs, new lives. My parents, my sisters and I went back to 'normality'. My father began a new job for an export com-pany, my mother was a housewife once again. My younger sister and I went back to school, while my older sister returned to her work as an apprentice dressmaker. Yet we had seen things no one should have seen, experienced things no one should have experienced and grown up ahead of our time. That word 'lucky' kept on appearing in my mind. I had heard stories of Austrians forcing Jews to scrub the pavement while they watched, laughed and sneered. They daubed Jewish shops with racist graffiti and murdered Jews. Fortunately I had not met those Austrians. There are, literally, thousands of tons of evidence: eyewitness accounts, photographic evidence, legal documents, to name a few. There is no denial of these facts, this terror, and no exoneration. I had met Austrians and Germans who would have killed me, given half the chance. So many of my aunts, uncles and cousins had been killed in Auschwitz. Yet it would be stupid if not prejudiced to believe that everyone in a single nation is inherently evil. All Germans were not Nazis, neither were all Austrians. There was opposition to the Nazi government – thousands of political prisoners in Germany proved that. Sadly they were the exception to the rule, as were those townspeople who were prepared to help in Mistelbach, a small town in the corner of an evil empire.

The large numbers of townspeople in Mistelbach who had helped my family, me and the others at the Forstgarten barracks did not have the courage to speak out aloud. They dared not and could not stop the Nazi apparatus; they could only try for moral and humane reasons, to alleviate the hardship of some of its victims. Yet their inconspicuous help showed their opposition to the treatment of their fellow man. The tragedy was that their example was an untypical show of dissent, inconspicuous or otherwise, in a most terrible war against such a wicked regime.